The 90-Minute Bitcoin Quick Start

The No-Nonsense Guide to Getting Started Quickly With Bitcoin and Cryptocurrency

James L. Paris

The 90-Minute Bitcoin Quick Start: The No-Nonsense Guide to Getting Started Quickly With Bitcoin and Cryptocurrency

Published by Bitcoin Bloodhound Publishing.

James Paris LLC, 250 Palm Coast Parkway #607-223 Palm Coast, FL 32137

For Permissions Contact:
Editorial@BitcoinbloodHound.com

Disclaimer: The author owns Bitcoin, Ethereum, Bitcoin Cash, Litecoin, and dozens of other cryptocurrencies discussed in this book. As a result, this analysis should not be relied upon as independent of conflicts of interests.

Before making any investment in digital currency, the reader should consult with a licensed financial adviser. This book should not be considered personalized advice, or a recommendation to buy or sell any cryptocurrencies or securities. Investing in cryptocurrencies is highly speculative in nature - YOU MAY LOSE YOUR ENTIRE INVESTMENT. Taxation of cryptocurrency is a complex matter, and readers should consult with their own tax adviser to determine their tax liability. The author is not a licensed financial adviser, and does not offer cryptocurrency for sale, advisory services, coaching, or any other financial consulting arrangements.

The regulation of cryptocurrency varies from state to state. Each state and country has unique regulatory restrictions. The author is not an attorney, and the contents of this book should not be construed as legal advice. Consult an attorney regarding the regulation of cryptocurrencies in your state or country.

The author specifically disclaims any and all liability from the application of the information contained in this book.

FTC Affiliate Disclosure: The author receives affiliate compensation from some links to products and services referenced in this book.

For more information, social media links, and other resources available from the author, visit BitcoinBloodhound.com.

James L. Paris is an early adopter of Bitcoin and founder of BitcoinBloodHound.com. He made his first purchase of Bitcoin in 2012. Paris is the author of more than thirty books, including *Living Financially Free, Money Management for Those Who Don't Have Any, The 100 Best Investments for Your Retirement,* and *Exposing the Ponzi Masters.* He is a graduate of the College for Financial Planning and has owned and operated a wide array of financial firms, including a nationwide broker-dealer and investment adviser, a mortgage brokerage, a real estate brokerage, and a publishing company. He has participated in the public and private securities offerings of more than 100 companies, and worked for more than a decade as a private portfolio manager.

Paris presently hosts *Jim Paris Live*, a nationwide radio show on the Genesis Communications Network (JimParisRadio.com). Paris has been a "regular" in national and worldwide financial media for more than three decades, appearing on a wide variety of well-known programs and media outlets, including Fox News Channel, The 700 Club, Coast To Coast AM, Daystar Television, Moody Radio Network, and countless others. Prior to hosting his own syndicated television show and numerous national radio broadcasts, he was the regular guest host of the nationwide Charles J. Givens radio program. He also served as a financial commentator for the Orlando CBS affiliate in the late 1980s.

Paris is a third-degree black in Taekwondo, a women's self-defense instructor, NRA firearms instructor, and an accomplished trumpet player. Jim has been married to his wife, Ann, for 31 years. They have three adult children and two dogs, and live in Palm Coast, Florida.

Dedication

To my grandfather, Carmen J. Paris. A survivor of the Normandy Invasion, and a recipient of the Bronze Star and the Purple Heart. Your example of how to live and love will never be forgotten. You will be greatly missed Pops.

Table of Contents

- ✓ 90-Minute Bitcoin Quick Start Updates
- ✓ Free E-Mail Newsletter
- ✓ News
- ✓ Videos
- ✓ Blog
- ✓ Recommended Links
- ✓ Market Commentary
- ✓ Educational Resources
- ✓ Market Analysis
- ✓ Discussion
- ✓ Q and A
- ✓ And More!

Preface: Welcome To The World Of Cryptocurrency

If you are a newcomer to cryptocurrency, hold on to your hat and buckle your seatbelt, as Mr. Toad's Wild Ride is about to begin. We are at that same moment as in the movie *The Matrix*, when Laurence Fishburne says:

"You take the blue pill — the story ends, you wake up in your bed and believe whatever you want to believe. You take the red pill — you stay in Wonderland, and I show you how deep the rabbit hole goes. Remember: all I'm offering is the truth."

Welcome to ***The 90-Minute Bitcoin Quick Start***. I will be your guide through the captivating world of digital money. To begin our journey, we must go back in time to 2009 when an unknown computer programmer by the name of Satoshi Nakamoto launched a new digital currency called Bitcoin (and note that we *still* don't know who Nakamoto is, or even if that's his real name).

The concept of digital money dates back to 1983, when software engineer David Chaum published a research paper on Digital Cash. Chaum was unable to execute on his idea, and the 'DigiCash' project went bankrupt in 1998. A year later,

PayPal was born, providing a platform for consumers to make the first generation of peer-to-peer payments. The mid- to late-nineties also saw the launch of something called E-Gold, which was digital money actually backed by physical gold. Although E-Gold begins to gain widespread acceptance, it is eventually shut down by regulators when it's found the new currency has become a favorite tool of criminals. Over the next ten years, several other now-forgotten digital currency upstarts suffer similar regulatory fates, including WebMoney, Liberty Reserve, and Perfect Money.

The Golden Rule

You may be familiar with the modern-day take on the Golden Rule: 'He who has the gold rules.' THE PRIMARY MEANS BY WHICH GOVERNMENTS CONTROL THEIR CITIZENS TODAY IS THROUGH THE MONETARY SYSTEM. Make no mistake about it - this is the real reason digital money is such a top priority for regulators. Enforcement actions against cryptocurrency are always justified as necessary to prevent money laundering and other financial crimes. We now know, however, that after the U.S. government shut down the so-called 'Silk Road,' there was little change in the volume of crypto transactions.

Bottom line: There is no empirical evidence that

criminals are using cryptocurrency in any greater percentage than they use good ol' cash. Painting all cryptocurrency users as criminals is a tired tactic, but one still aggressively applied by governments and regulators worldwide.

2008 - The Money Revolution Begins

We remain in the midst of a worldwide financial revolution that began ten years ago. People everywhere have decided they're ready to leave the corrupt and archaic global monetary system.

The financial crimes and mismanagement leading to the 2008 financial collapse were epic. Even more consequential was the U.S. government's decision that the unscrupulous financial institutions behind the disaster were 'too big to fail,' and therefore worthy of receiving unfathomable sums of taxpayer money. You may recall that rumblings of the coming crisis began as the subprime mortgage market started to implode, but the financial earthquake of a generation officially struck the global financial system on September 15, 2008 with the collapse of Lehman Brothers.

Despite widespread financial mismanagement, reprehensible risk taking, and outright fraud, only one banker went to prison. While billions in phony assets disappeared from financial ledgers,

Uncle Sam was left to pick up the pieces. A small handful of financial executives were given slaps on the wrist by the justice system, while many more bailed out of the industry altogether, their landings greatly softened by obscene, multi-million-dollar golden parachutes.

2009 - The Launch Of Bitcoin

The 2008 disintegration of billions in phantom assets created the perfect moment for a worldwide epiphany. WHILE MANY DIGITAL MONEY CONCEPTS HAD COME AND GONE, THERE WAS SOMETHING VERY DIFFERENT AND SPECIAL ABOUT BITCOIN: IT WOULD BE THE FIRST DECENTRALIZED DIGITAL CURRENCY. Unlike its predecessors, Bitcoin would operate without a centralized computer network, office, or even a physical location. It was an entirely virtual operation. Trying to shut it down would be like chasing a ghost. And if not for its decentralized structure, Bitcoin would surely have been chased from existence.

Another Shot In The Arm To Crypto - The 2013 Cyprus Bail-In

In March 2013, the Republic of Cyprus (an island nation near the coast of Greece) enacted a levy on all uninsured bank deposits. The term 'bail-in' was coined to describe the confiscation of millions of dollars used to rescue the small country from total financial collapse.

In a story connecting the Cyprus bail-in to the rise of Bitcoin, CNN Money noted:

"Bitcoin is an unusual place to seek security. It's a four-year-old digital currency developed by a hacker who remains anonymous... the price of one Bitcoin has popped 87% since Cyprus began discussing tapping deposits as part of the bailout by the EU and IMF. Bitcoin now trade at $88 each, up from $47 on March 16, 2013 according to data from Mt. Gox, the currency's main trading exchange. That compares with just 5 cents per Bitcoin in mid-July 2010, when Mt. Gox first started tracking prices."

In my view, the Cyprus bail-in put Bitcoin on the map, including on the radar of governments worldwide. Those smart enough to migrate their money out of the banking system and into the Bitcoin lifeboat were able escape the massive confiscation.

THIS SINGLE EVENT DEMONSTRATED HOW POWERLESS GOVERNMENTS WERE AGAINST THIS NEW KIND OF MONEY. BITCOIN SUDDENLY BECAME A PHENOMENON. IT WAS A 'THING,' AND IT'S CLEAR THE DAM WAS STARTING TO BREAK. THE LITTLE GUY FINALLY HAD

SOMETHING: A POWERFUL TOOL THAT HE COULD USE TO PROTECT HIS CHICKENS FROM THE WOLVES - IT WAS TRULY A *SHOT HEARD 'ROUND THE WORLD!*

Is Bitcoin Really Anonymous?

This may be one of the most misunderstood features of Bitcoin. Although frequently compared to a Swiss bank account, BITCOIN IS NOT ACTUALLY ANONYMOUS - IT IS *PSEUDONYMOUS*. This is because it operates on a public ledger system. THE HISTORY OF EACH AND EVERY BITCOIN TRANSACTION THAT HAS EVER OCCURRED IS PUBLICLY AVAILABLE. Anyone can download the entire transaction history of Bitcoin back to the very beginning (the so-called 'Genesis block'). From the public ledger, wallet addresses can be used to track individual transactions. While the transactions are not anonymous, the owner of the wallet address *is* (at least for now).

Amazon presently has a patent pending for a technology they claim will completely 'unmask' the identity of all Bitcoin users. They plan to profit by selling this data to law enforcement. NSA whistle-blower Edward Snowden recently tweeted that the government has been monitoring Bitcoin users for several years. Crypto privacy is going to be a never-ending arms race, as programmers on both sides feverishly develop countermeasures to one another.

Why You Should Care About Your Financial Privacy

Later in this book, I will provide a complete overview of cryptocurrency wallets, and a simple strategy that can be used to enhance anonymity. There is a myriad of reasons to keep your financial affairs private. The media wants to boil down the desire for financial privacy to tax evasion, money laundering, and other nefarious activity, but this unequivocally misses the point. GOVERNMENT TRACKING OF ITS CITIZENS' DETAILED FINANCIAL TRANSACTIONS IS NOT JUST INTRUSIVE, BUT REPRESENTS *A MONUMENTAL DIMINISHMENT OF OUR CONSTITUTIONAL RIGHTS*.

Do you want the government monitoring what books you read? Where you spend your day? What your religious views are? Your political leanings? How many firearms you own? Only those ignorant of history say things like "If you have nothing to hide, why be concerned about the government looking into your private affairs?" The Fourth Amendment to the Constitution may be our most valuable right:

"The right of the people to be secure in their persons, houses, papers, and effects, against unreasonable searches and seizures, shall not be

violated, and no Warrants shall issue, but upon probable cause, supported by Oath or affirmation, and particularly describing the place to be searched, and the persons or things to be seized."

While the framers could not anticipate the role technology would play in destroying individual privacy, the Fourth Amendment still stands today as a bedrock of the unique rights we enjoy as Americans. The loss of privacy (financial and otherwise) ultimately leads to a devastating erosion of personal freedom.

The Financial Deep-State Conspiracy Against Cryptocurrency

In the beginning of 2018, social media giant Facebook suddenly announced a blanket ban on cryptocurrency advertising. This ban extended beyond crypto itself, applying even to books and educational courses. It was an indiscriminate and overly broad move that has left more than a few people wondering what the real agenda is.

While defended as a needed protection against ICO (initial coin offering) scams, the folks at Facebook used a sledgehammer rather than a scalpel to get the job done. ICOs could have simply been banned or restricted, but Facebook decided instead to light a match to the entire cryptocurrency space.

There are, after all, plenty of investment scams out there; why hasn't Facebook taken the same broad approach and banned all ads on day trading, real estate flipping, options trading, annuities, Internet marketing, and insurance products? These supposedly 'legitimate' areas within the realm of personal finance are all riddled with scams of their own.

Then there are the high-profile financial personalities who have been very outspoken in their disdain for the cryptocurrency markets, from JPMorgan chairman Jamie Dimon, to Warren Buffett, to former Wells Fargo CEO Dick Kovacevich, who went as far as to call Bitcoin a pyramid scheme (I will get to my thoughts on the precarious moral high ground of Wells Fargo in a moment). What's more, earlier this year, Bank of America, Chase, and Citibank all instituted bans on cryptocurrency purchases with credit cards.

Speaking of Bank of America, here is an example of in just how much contempt the institution holds cryptocurrency:

According to a recent news item, *the banking giant decided to close the account of a three-year-old because her father is a hedge fund manager who invests in the crypto markets.*

THE REPORT DETAILS THAT THERE WAS NO CRYPTOCURRENCY ACTIVITY IN THE FAMILY'S (OR THE TODDLER'S) ACCOUNTS AT THE BANK, BUT THE FATHER'S PROFESSIONAL INVOLVEMENT WITH CRYPTOCURRENCY RESULTED IN THE ENTIRE FAMILY BEING PROHIBITED FROM DOING ANY FURTHER BUSINESS WITH BANK OF AMERICA.

Beware Of The Financial Deep State

What is the real agenda here? I certainly don't believe it's about financial institutions protecting their customers. It is also not about wise old financial legends merely offering what they earnestly believe to be sage advice. These are robber barons doing everything within their power to stop the peasants from venturing outside the city walls. THE FINANCIAL DEEP STATE AND WORLD GOVERNMENTS HAVE FORMED AN UNHOLY ALLIANCE TO PREVENT THE MASSES FROM ATTAINING TRUE FINANCIAL FREEDOM.

Think about it: These are the very people who get a little piece (and sometimes even a *big* piece) of every dollar we earn, spend, and invest. THIS IS A WAR TEN THOUSAND TIMES BIGGER THAN BREXIT, AND FAR MORE CONSEQUENTIAL.

IMAGINE A WORLD WHERE EACH PERSON COULD POSSESS AND MOVE MONEY FREELY WITHOUT

INTERMEDIARIES; A WORLD WHERE GOVERNMENTS HAVE NO MEANS TO CONFISCATE THE FUNDS OF THEIR CITIZENS. DECENTRALIZATION WILL STRIP THE ELITES OF UNTOLD TRILLIONS OF DOLLARS IN GENERATIONAL WEALTH. MORE THAN A NEW RENAISSANCE, IT WILL BE THE GREATEST SHIFT OF POWER IN THE HISTORY OF THE WORLD.

The age-old mantra 'follow the money' could not fit more perfectly. This battle is not really against cryptocurrency, per se, but decentralization. Just like with Brexit, I predict that efforts to stop the movement will ultimately fail. Each financial Obi-Wan who issues their own dire warning on Bitcoin may rock the markets for a day or two, but ONCE THE MASSES REALIZE THAT THESE WARNINGS ARE COMPLETELY SELF-SERVING, THEY WILL BECOME MEANINGLESS.

The REAL WARNING You Should Be Concerned About

Why is there no warning about the U.S. government's own Ponzi schemes? Consider the collapse of 2008, the bankrupt pension systems across this country, the incalculable risk of the derivatives markets, or the mother of all financially rigged schemes, Social Security. How can anyone with a straight face warn about Bitcoin while there is more than $200 trillion dollars of debt and unfunded liabilities on the books of the federal government? IF ANYONE IS TAKING AN OUTRAGEOUS RISK HERE, IT IS THOSE INDIVIDUALS THAT DON'T HAVE AT LEAST A PORTION OF THEIR MONEY OUTSIDE THE U.S. FINANCIAL SYSTEM.

When I see the likes of Warren Buffett warning Americans about Bitcoin, I ask where Mr. Buffet was to warn us when Wells Fargo was opening thousands of bogus accounts at the expense of their customers? Lo and behold, during what was one of the biggest 'scams' in the banking industry since the 2008 mortgage meltdown, it turns out that Berkshire Hathaway was the largest shareholder in Wells Fargo. And as one deep-state financial scandal is eclipsed by the next, I only see golden parachutes and meaningless fines - not handcuffs. After the legendary 'fake account' scandal, Wells Fargo CEO John Stump left the company with a $130-million-dollar retirement package.

Cryptocurrency Is Supposedly A Risky Scam, But Now The Elites All Want In On It

- It was just reported that Facebook has been researching the development of its own cryptocurrency for over a year now.
- JPMorgan (Jamie Dimon’s firm) just

announced that they are also doing their own research on Bitcoin and that it will "play a role" in the future.

- Warren Buffett recently upped his criticism, calling Bitcoin "rat poison squared." However, we now know that his own BNSF Railroad just implemented use of the blockchain!
- Bank of America was just granted a patent for a cryptocurrency and trading platform of its own.
- National cryptocurrencies are almost here. There have been serious discussions about a so-called E-Dollar that would be created by the U.S. Treasury. Switzerland just announced plans to develop its own national cryptocurrency (the E-Franc). I just spent a week in Switzerland. They are fiercely independent (which is why they are not a member of the European Union) and committed to becoming a major player in cryptocurrency.

Introduction: My Cryptocurrency Journey

It's the spring of 2018 and I am making small talk at a cocktail party in a room of septuagenarians. It was a gathering of your typical country club blue bloods. Nice fellows, but they were frozen in time, like characters right out of a black and white movie. A man with a booming voice that came from across the room asked, "What do you do for a living?" "I write financial books," I sheepishly answered. "Well, what financial book are you writing now?" he inquired. To which I replied, "My current book is on Bitcoin and cryptocurrency."

At that moment, it was as if I'd announced that I was infected with the Ebola virus. I still get a good laugh thinking about the exchange. Jaws hit the floor when I added that I was also an *investor* in cryptocurrency. Apparently, I had just lit a bomb and thrown it into the middle of the room. No one was rude enough to outright laugh at me, but I could see them biting their lips to hold it in. The conversation ended with, "Well son, you must have a big set on you to be buying that stuff."

My Accidental Adventure Into The World Of Cryptocurrency

In October 2012 I purchased $20 of Bitcoin as research for an article I was writing about digital money. At that time, Bitcoin was just $12. My original $20 gave me 1.7 Bitcoins. I spent some of that original Bitcoin, but held on to one coin. My son, in college at the time, asked if he could buy in. I agreed, and we became 50/50 partners in the one Paris family Bitcoin. AT THE TIME, IT ALL SEEMED SO TRIVIAL; NEVER DID WE THINK THAT OUR TINY BITCOIN INVESTMENT WOULD END UP APPROACHING A VALUE OF ALMOST $10,000 EACH (DECEMBER 2017) WHEN BITCOIN NEARLY HIT $20,000!

My second experience with crypto involved Ripple XRP. I heard a talk show discussing it, and I was intrigued with what was being described as 'digital money for the banking system.' I was also attracted by the price, which was less than a penny at the time. I came up with the idea of buying Ripple and giving it away as a bonus to subscribers of my financial newsletter. It was an immediate hit. I would give a new subscriber anywhere from 500 to 1,000 Ripple coins as a sign-up bonus. Although my original intent was to buy it for myself, I ended up giving it away as fast as I bought it. JUST AS WITH BITCOIN, I REGRET NOT BUYING MORE, AS RIPPLE XRP RECENTLY HIT

$3.65 IN JANUARY 2018.

The world of cryptocurrency is filled with so many stories like mine. AS MUCH AS I WISH I COULD GO BACK IN TIME AND HAVE INVESTED MORE, I HONESTLY BELIEVE THAT THESE ARE STILL THE VERY EARLY DAYS OF THE DIGITAL MONEY REVOLUTION.

My goal in writing this get-started guide is to give you the action steps you need so you won't have your own regrets five years from now. Maybe you can envision yourself someday sharing your own Bitcoin financial success story with a grandchild - it is fun to think in those terms. I have also had a good laugh imagining how *another* story might be shared by a grandparent who sat on the sidelines during the digital currency revolution: "Johnny, if grandpa had only bought Bitcoin when it was $10,000 a few years back, I could pay cash for your college education and buy your first house for you."

By the way, in this book, I use the terms 'cryptocurrency' and 'digital money' interchangeably (and sometimes I just say 'crypto'). Crypto purists might take issue with me for doing so, as there *are* some technical differences between the two. However, those distinctions aren't important to the mission at hand. In fact, simplicity is *intended* to be one of the features of ***The 90-Minute Bitcoin Quick Start.***

How Can Digital Money Be Worth Anything?

I find this question amusing because it is typically asked by people who are oblivious to the erosion of the value of the dollar. What gives a currency its value is a sensible question to ask, don't get me wrong; I guess we have all lived our entire lives accepting that rectangular pieces of paper in our pockets with pictures of dead presidents represent genuine value. But why *is* value attributed to the dollar? Since the end of the gold standard in 1971, the U.S. dollar has not been backed by anything (the technical term is 'fiat currency'). IT IS A COMPLETE MYTH THAT ITS VALUE IS SOMEHOW INSURED OR BACKED UP BY THE UNITED STATES GOVERNMENT.

Does The Government Actually Guarantee The Value Of The Dollar?

There is no government agency that promises a dollar in the future will buy the same goods and services it does today. The government accepts the dollar for the payment of taxes and has declared it to be legal tender, but that's it. Note this revealing quote from a research paper recently published by the St. Louis Federal Reserve: "Bitcoin is not the only currency that has no intrinsic value. State monopoly currencies, such as the U.S. dollar, the Euro, and the Swiss franc, have no intrinsic value either." WITH BITCOIN, YOU ARE PUTTING YOUR FAITH IN COMPUTER CODE, AND WITH THE DOLLAR, YOU ARE PUTTING YOUR CONFIDENCE IN A RECTANGULAR PIECE OF PAPER COMPOSED OF 25 PERCENT LINEN AND 75 PERCENT COTTON.

BITCOIN HAS A VALUE BECAUSE A GROUP OF PEOPLE HAVE AGREED TO ACCEPT IT AS A MEANS OF EXCHANGE. It is as simple as that. This basis for ascribing value to mediums of exchange goes back to ancient times, when people used a wide variety of objects as currency, including rare stones, gold, silver, copper, and even seashells. Anything can be a medium of exchange if two people agree that it is.

Why Bitcoin Has Real Value

However, Bitcoin has more than mere psychology going for it as justification for being seen as a store of value. First, there will only be a total of 21 million coins ever created (at the time this book was published, there are only 4 million coins remaining to be mined). Contrast this to the United States' 'elastic' money supply, and you can easily see the value proposition. Because it exists in a finite supply, BITCOIN IS A BONA FIDE CURRENCY THAT WILL NOT ONLY HOLD ITS VALUE

OVER TIME, BUT *APPRECIATE*.

The Falling Value Of The Dollar

Want to try an enlightening exercise? Spend a few minutes at InflationCalculator.com. If you do, you will learn that a typical $1 item in 1950 will cost you $10.35 today! I think most adults are generally aware that a dollar doesn't go as far as it used to, but you might be surprised at just how much the purchasing power of money has diminished under the fiat currency system. Retirees today frequently share anecdotes about how a gallon of gas cost just 18 cents in 1950, or a loaf of bread could be had for just a quarter in 1970.

In other countries, the level of inflation is downright extraordinary. For example, in Venezuela, inflation recently hit an annual rate of 13,800 percent! There are no words to describe how bad things have become for Venezuelans after the complete collapse of their currency. Hundreds of thousands of citizens have fled the country, many ending up in Ecuador. A LOCAL RESIDENT OF ECUADOR SHARED WITH ME THE STORY OF A FORMER VENEZUELAN MEDICAL DOCTOR WORKING THERE AS A HOUSE CLEANER, EARNING BARELY ENOUGH MONEY FOR FOOD.

Besides existing in a finite supply, Bitcoin has

other features that enhance its intrinsic value, like the blockchain. The blockchain represents a true technological innovation. We won't get into too much detail here about the blockchain; suffice it to say, it is a system of record-keeping that uses so-called 'blocks.' These blocks (records) are connected, so that an accurate history of transactions can be recorded. Since each transaction is linked as a chain within a history of other records, *it represents a tamper-proof public ledger*. The concept is simple, yet so ingenious, that its implementation and use is burgeoning within both government and private industry (notably, within the medical field).

Bitcoin offers another tremendous advantage: it is decentralized. Decentralization means the currency can be held and transacted without an intermediary. LIKE CASH, BITCOIN CAN BE IN YOUR POSSESSION AND STORED WITHOUT BEING 'ON DEPOSIT' WITH A BANK OR FINANCIAL INSTITUTION. THIS PROVIDES INCREASED PRIVACY AND AN ASSET THAT CAN BE BOTH PORTABLE AND SECURE.

Because Bitcoin is digital and decentralized, it can be sent directly from one person to another (peer-to-peer) without a middleman. If you have ever experienced the headache of wiring money internationally, or dealt with the cost of using Western Union, you can immediately see how revolutionary Bitcoin is. A friend of mine is the head of a large organization that sends wires overseas to missionary projects. A WIRE FROM THE UNITED STATES TO AN INTERNATIONAL ACCOUNT WILL TYPICALLY TAKE SEVERAL DAYS TO SHOW UP! COMPARE THAT TO BITCOIN, WHICH CAN BE SENT DIRECTLY TO ANYONE IN THE WORLD AND RECEIVED IN JUST MINUTES!

The ability to remit funds from one person to another directly *and* worldwide is a real game-changer. How much do people pay every day just to access and spend their own money? Monthly account fees, wire fees, credit card fees, low balance fees, overdraft charges, and ATM fees are just some of the expenses we have to absorb solely for the 'privilege' of using our own money. MAKE NO MISTAKE: WHAT IS HAPPENING WITH CRYPTOCURRENCY IS REVOLUTIONARY.

Of course, this book is about much more than just Bitcoin. With the advent of each new cryptocurrency, we see greater innovation. Although many analysts regularly brand new cryptos as Bitcoin 2.0, THE TRUTH IS THAT THERE WILL NEVER BE ANOTHER BITCOIN. IT WAS THE FIRST BLOCKCHAIN-BASED CRYPTOCURRENCY, AND ESTABLISHED THE PROTOCOLS AND PARAMETERS BY WHICH ALL OTHERS WILL BE JUDGED.

Can Bitcoin Be Dethroned?

Many are predicting that we will eventually see a so-called 'flippening,' which will be the day that Bitcoin is surpassed in market capitalization by another coin. Current favorites to potentially knock Bitcoin from the top spot include Ethereum and Ripple. While I don't think this is an impossible scenario, if it happens, it would be tantamount to slaying a dragon. Bitcoin has an enormous head start, and benefits immensely from its 'first mover advantage' and worldwide adoption levels.

What Is The Potential Future Price Of Bitcoin?

I have had guests on my radio show predict Bitcoin's future value to be anywhere from $100,000 to $2 million. Roger Ver, a well-known Bitcoin investor and advocate, appeared as a guest in February 2016 and prophesied Bitcoin would eventually surpass $1 million (this was before the advent of the Bitcoin Cash 'hard fork,' to which Ver moved his support). If you want to listen to the complete interview with Ver, search Google for "Jim Paris Live Roger Ver." Famed software creator John McAfee is also forecasting a price point for Bitcoin of $1 million by 2020. ONE OF THE FOUNDERS OF PAYPAL, PETER THIEL, WHO RECENTLY INVESTED MILLIONS OF DOLLARS IN BITCOIN, COMPARED IT TO DIGITAL GOLD.

In order to formulate a realistic estimate of Bitcoin's ultimate future value, there are many variables to consider. But when you realize a single Bitcoin worth less than a penny in 2009 now has a value of thousands of dollars, the possibilities seem practically limitless.

A commodity with a limited supply and increasing demand is going to continue to appreciate in value. THAT PRINCIPLE IS ECONOMICS 101. ACCORDINGLY, WHILE I WON'T OFFER MY OWN PRICE PREDICTION HERE, A MILLION-DOLLAR OR EVEN TWO-MILLION-DOLLAR BITCOIN WOULD NOT SURPRISE ME.

The Fast Track Plan To Your First Bitcoin Purchase

I have gone back and forth on how large this book should be and how much information it should contain. I've decided on a 'happy medium,' wanting to provide a solid overview of the subject without allowing the text to become burdensome. In that spirit, consider this section the 'Fast Track Plan' to your first Bitcoin Purchase. I don't want you to feel as though you must read every single page of this book before you get started on your own cryptocurrency journey. I HAVE PLANNED THIS BOOK TO BE BOTH A QUICK-START GUIDE *AND* A PRACTICAL A-TO-Z

REFERENCE. USE THE ACTION PLAN BELOW TO GET STARTED QUICKLY, AND READ THE BALANCE OF THE BOOK AT YOUR OWN PACE. **While there is another lengthier section on buying crypto (including alternatives to Bitcoin), the abbreviated version below is an express lane to your first PURCHASE.**

1. Decide How Much Money You Want To Initially Invest

As mentioned earlier, I started my cryptocurrency journey with $20. That might be the right amount for you, but only invest an amount that you can afford to lose.

Also, don't balk at investing in Bitcoin because you cannot afford the cost one full Bitcoin. You can absolutely buy less than a full Bitcoin. As a matter of fact, Bitcoin is divisible by up to 8 digits past the decimal point (example 0.1234567). This means you can buy very tiny amounts (one hundred millionth – also nicknamed a 'Satoshi'). To make the math easy, if Bitcoin is trading at $10,000 and you invest $100, you will own 1 percent of a Bitcoin, or .01.

Almost all cryptos can be bought and sold fractionally in this same manner. The divisibility of Bitcoin is a key feature that makes it spendable, even if the value of one coin becomes worth tens of millions of dollars.

2. Select A Platform To Make Your Purchase

Several purchase platforms are discussed later in this book, but I strongly recommend Coinbase for newbies. It is easy to use and there is no minimum. Use my referral link (BitcoinBonus.US) and receive $10 of free Bitcoin with your first $100 purchase (offer subject to change). COINBASE AND THE OTHER OPTIONS LISTED BELOW ARE SIMPLE BUYING PLATFORMS, *NOT* CRYPTOCURRENCY EXCHANGES. Wait until you have finished reading this book in its entirety before trading at a crypto exchange. Crypto exchanges provide more options for investors using advanced trading strategies (more on exchanges in Section Four).

Other Simple Buying Platforms:

- CoinMama
- Square Cash
- Uphold
- BitPanda
- Robinhood

3. Install The App

Most buying platforms today involve the use of an app. For example, while Coinbase does have a website, most of its core functions are available exclusively through the app. Depending on what platform you use, the associated app will have varying degrees of importance. In some cases, the app may contain the vital functions of the platform, while other apps may just serve as a mobile version of the website. Even if the app is just a secondary means of tracking your account, it is worth taking a minute to download it to your mobile device. IN THE CASE OF COINBASE (AND ROBINHOOD), THE APP IS A NECESSITY.

4. Carefully Select Your Security Options When Setting Up Your Account

Whether you use Coinbase or an alternative, be sure to take full advantage of all available security measures. Although two-factor authentication may not be required, I highly recommend it. The easiest form of two-factor authentication involves the SMS (text message). The mechanism triggers a text with a newly generated password for the second step of your log-in. Two-step authentication is a good habit to form right from the start, even though you might only make a modest initial deposit.

5. Get Ready For Verification

To comply with anti-money laundering laws and other government regulations, you will have to prove your identity. How this is precisely done will vary from one platform to the next, but having to provide a copy of your driver's license or passport is standard (also, your Social Security number, birth date, and address will be required).

There was a time, not too long ago, that such rigid identification measures weren't required to open a crypto account. Many new investors are understandably concerned about sharing such information online, especially with all the recent data hacks, but it's just the same kind of information that's required when opening a bank or brokerage account.

Something else to be aware of: Verification is not always a smooth process. Depending on network traffic and other factors, you might have to submit and *re-submi*t your information a few times before it is fully processed. While this can be frustrating, know that it is not uncommon.

6. Fund Your Account

You now have a shiny new account at your selected Bitcoin buying platform. The next step is getting money into the account to make your first purchase. Until recently, the easiest way to fund an account was with a credit card, but the major credit card companies started banning Bitcoin purchases in early 2018. Even with the credit card ban, some debit cards can still be used. The best alternative to credit/debit cards is an ACH deposit (transfer from your checking or savings). An ACH deposit can take up to seven business days to fully transact.

Payment Methods for US Customers

There are several types of payment methods that you can link to your Coinbase account:

	Best for	Buy	Sell	Deposit	Withdraw	Speed
Bank Account (ACH)	Large and small investments	✓	✓	✓	✓	4-5 business days
Debit Card	Small investments	✓	X	X	X	Instant
Wire Transfer	Large investments	X	X	✓	✓	1-3 business days

7. Make Your Purchase

Once you receive a notification that you have money in your account, you will need to log in and complete your purchase. There can be some confusion about this final step. REMEMBER, ONCE YOUR ACCOUNT IS FUNDED, YOU STILL HAVE TO INITIATE A SEPARATE PURCHASE TRANSACTION IN ORDER TO ACTUALLY BUY BITCOIN OR OTHER DIGITAL CURRENCY.

What Now?

You might be the first kid on your block to own Bitcoin, but now what? Making a small Bitcoin purchase is just the BEGINNING of your journey. Curiosity will lead you deeper and deeper into the crypto jungle. On that note, I felt it was important to get right down to business and not wait until the end of this book to change your status from 'crypto observer' to 'crypto owner.' As I say to my martial arts students, you now have your white belt; now the *real* training begins!

Here's a brief overview of what's next:

Section 1 - Why You Don't Need To Completely Understand Cryptocurrency To Own It

'Analysis paralysis' is the number one reason most people remain spectators and never actually enter the cryptocurrency arena. How much do you really need to know about the inner workings of digital currency to make your first purchase?

Section 2 – How To Send And Receive Cryptocurrency

Now that you have entered the crypto world, you will need to learn how to safely send and receive digital currency.

Section 3 - The Care And Feeding Of Your Cryptocurrency

It may not be as big of a responsibility as parenting a child, but your cryptocurrency portfolio *will* require ongoing attention. You'll want to be familiar with the wide range of crypto security measures available, and this section will be your guide about how to defend yourself from online and offline thieves. We will also explore the various wallets available to hold your cryptocurrency.

Section 4 - Buying Cryptocurrency 2.0

In the beginning of this book, I provide you with a very basic plan on how to bag your first cryptocurrency within just ninety minutes. Consider this section your *2.0* guide to buying Bitcoin and alt-coins.

Section 5 - What Kind Of Crypto Investor Will You Be?

Crystalize your vision and strategy by deciding what kind of crypto investor you want to be. Will you buy and hold your digital currency, or trade the markets? Will you set your sights exclusively on the bigger-name coins, or will you also search for diamonds among the upstarts? Will you be investing in a lump sum, or spread your purchases over a period of weeks or months?

Section 6 - Following The Action

Cryptocurrency trades 24 hours a day, 7 days a week. How will you follow events, your coins, and the market action? Where will you get your news, ongoing education, and investment ideas?

Section 7 - My Crypto Hot List

Until you develop your own short list of favorites, you can start by borrowing mine. Some names will be familiar, other less so, and you'll even find an idea or two pulled from left field for your consideration.

Section 8 - How To Spend Bitcoin

This is where you'll find retailers that accept cryptocurrency. You'll even learn how to save up to 33 percent on Amazon purchases when you pay with Bitcoin.

Section 9 - Bitcoin Comes To Wall Street

This section provides an overview of the Grayscale Bitcoin Trust (known as 'Bitcoin Stock'), discusses how to purchase Bitcoin within an IRA, and addresses the future of Bitcoin in the securities markets.

Section 10 - Get Your Crypto For Free

Here you'll learn how to build your crypto holdings without spending a dime of your own money. This section contains a wealth of information on subjects such as the top affiliate programs, accepting crypto as payment for *your* professional services, exchanging your Amazon Associates earnings for Bitcoin, earning crypto for blog and video posts, crypto mining, and even accepting crypto as a donation or tip from your followers.

Section One: Why You Don't Need To Completely Understand Cryptocurrency To Own It

I remember a time, not too many years ago, when it was seen as cute for people to announce that they were 'computer illiterate.' Just a relative handful of years later, however, proclaiming your lack of computer skills is no longer a laughing matter. Basic computer competence is now just as important as being able to read, and an essential requirement in most workplaces.

It's 1995 In The World Of Cryptocurrency

There are too many parallels to list here between the adoption of the Internet and the adoption of cryptocurrency. Similar to the reaction when the Internet first became publicly accessible, Bitcoin-deniers laugh hysterically and loudly declare that they have no idea what Bitcoin is, that they'll never understand it, and that they'll NEVER BUY ANY. No doubt, many of these same people once said they would never own a home computer, use the Internet, have a Facebook account, and so on. The so-called 'Internet *adoption curve*' mirrors the growth rate of cryptocurrency rather remarkably - COMPARED TO INTERNET

ADOPTION, WE ARE STILL ONLY IN 1995 IN TERMS OF CRYPTOCURRENCY'S EVOLUTION. JUST IMAGINE WHERE CYPTOCURRENCY – AND YOU – WILL BE IN ANOTHER 20 TO 25 YEARS.

% of American adults (ages 18+) who use the internet, over time. As of May 2013, 85% of adults use the internet.

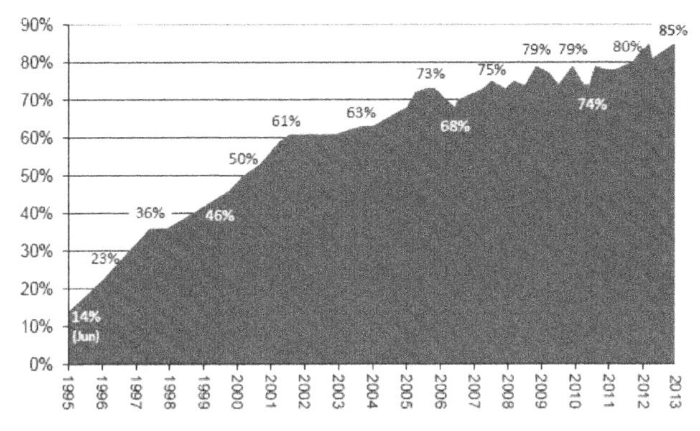

Source: Pew Research Surveys, 1995-May 2013.
More: http://pewinternet.org/Trend-Data/Internet-Adoption.aspx

As noted, most experts believe we are still in the very early stages of the cryptocurrency adoption curve. In Internet adoption terms, we are at a point similar to where we were in the mid-1990s, when most businesses did not yet have a website and just a tiny percentage of the population was using the Internet.

How Much Do You Need To Know To Be A Crypto Investor?

Not as much as you may think. There are basically two broad components to crypto: *cryptography*, which has to do with the software and programming side of things, and what's called *use case*, which concerns the spending and investing of cryptocurrency. It is the latter component we will focus on in this book. I will concede that I've not spent much time studying the computer science behind crypto, but that's perfectly OK. YOU DON'T NEED TO BE A CRYPTOGRAPHY EXPERT TO USE AND INVEST IN CRYPTOCURRENCY.

Traditional Investing Wisdom Is Not A Good Fit Here

We have all been warned about not investing in what we don't understand, right? Back in the day, when Peter Lynch was one of stock market investing's top guns, he made his name writing books and teaching that you should invest in businesses where you actually spend your money. For example, if your kids strong-armed you into buying a popular new athletic shoe, maybe you should consider also buying some stock in the company.

While I believe there *can* be wisdom to this

approach when it comes to buying stocks, it's not necessary to apply it, without fail, in every case. For example, there are so many great technology stocks that do things I will never fully grasp, and yet I still invest in them. This is because despite my lack of technical understanding of what the underlying companies do, the available information on their investment potential is very useful and actionable. It is this perspective that largely informs my decisions related to buying cryptocurrency, as well.

So Many Questions That My Head Was Spinning...

I had struggled with all the same questions everyone has when I started my crypto journey in 2012. How is this money? Why is it worth anything? Can it be hacked? Will this ever really catch on? Isn't this just for drug dealers and criminals? Will the government try to shut it down?

I ultimately decided that my focus should remain on the investment side of Bitcoin, and that I would leave the technical stuff to software geeks. In truth, fully understanding how a device or other mechanism works is not necessary in order for me to appreciate its value. I can't explain how my TV works, but I watch it. I use the Internet, a wide variety of computers and tablets, my smart phone, and so many other gadgets - all without being able to expertly dissect the technology behind them.

If becoming a cryptography expert is a prerequisite for you to get started in Bitcoin, you will likely miss the boat. There are plenty of books available that address the computer science component to digital currency. HOWEVER, *MY* GOAL IS TO GET YOU OUT OF THE SPECTATOR SEATS AND ON TO THE FIELD. DON'T GET BOGGED DOWN WITH 'ANALYSIS PARALYSIS.'

Section Two: How To Send And Receive Cryptocurrency

MY FIRST PIECE OF ADVICE TO YOU ON LEARNING TO SEND AND RECEIVE CRYPTOCURRENCY IS TO *START SMALL*. Have a friend or relative set up a Bitcoin wallet, and send them a tiny amount as a test. Once you learn the process, purchasing *any* digital money should be easy.

Sending and receiving crypto is very similar to sending and receiving e-mail. Within your wallet you will have a public 'receive address.' You can share this with others (just like you would an e-mail address). IF YOU EXPECT SOMEONE TO SEND YOU CRYPTOCURRENCY, THEY WILL NEED YOUR WALLET RECEIVE ADDRESS. NOTE, HOWEVER, THEY DO *NOT* NEED ANY OTHER DETAILS ABOUT YOUR ACCOUNT. Don't provide log-in credentials, private keys, or other information that could make your wallet vulnerable.

The address length and configuration will vary for different coins. For Bitcoin, most addresses will contain 34 characters (although older addresses have as few as 26 characters and are still valid). Take a few minutes and watch a couple of YouTube tutorials and you should have no problem mastering the send and receive process.

Use of the QR code can make transacting Bitcoin particularly easy. The QR code is a two-dimensional barcode that serves as a visual representation of a Bitcoin address. Wallet apps can access the camera on your mobile device to basically take a picture of the QR code and instantly import the address. For example, if I want to transfer Bitcoin from my Coinbase account, I can pull up the app, click on 'send' and the small QR code icon. After doing so, I point my phone at the QR code of the receiving wallet. The QR code is picked up by my phone's camera and then converted into the receiving wallet's alphanumeric address.

I don't want to overcomplicate things here, so the easiest way to understand QR codes is that they transfer the long 34-character address between computers. You can still use the 'old school' option of copying and pasting the addresses, but QR codes are much faster. Of course, when you manually type in a wallet address, it's easy to make an error, so that's not a good idea.

Example Of A QR Code

As cryptocurrency becomes ubiquitous, you will find QR codes available for payments at restaurants, coffee shops, retail stores, and even your doctor's office. In some parts of the country, the display of QR codes at merchant locations is already commonplace.

WARNING: A DESTINATION TAG MAY BE REQUIRED

Depending on the crypto you are sending or receiving, some of the exchanges MAY require a 'destination tag' when you transfer coins. This is very common when sending Ripple XRP. A destination tag is usually an eight-digit transaction reference number. If you forget to include this, you won't lose your coins, but it may take a few days for the transaction to be refunded back to you.

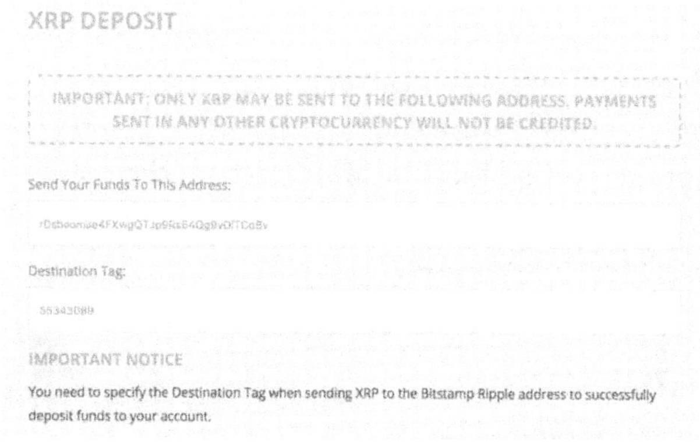

XRP DEPOSIT

IMPORTANT: ONLY XRP MAY BE SENT TO THE FOLLOWING ADDRESS. PAYMENTS SENT IN ANY OTHER CRYPTOCURRENCY WILL NOT BE CREDITED.

Send Your Funds To This Address:

Destination Tag:

IMPORTANT NOTICE

You need to specify the Destination Tag when sending XRP to the Bitstamp Ripple address to successfully deposit funds to your account.

Section Three: The Care And Feeding Of Your Cryptocurrency Holdings

While it is not imperative that you become a crypto expert before making your first purchase, you *will* need a grasp of the basics.

For starters, I want to address the matter of owning and holding digital money. When you make your first purchase, you won't receive anything physical (remember, this is a completely virtual asset). Like your bank account, you will see the purchase online. *Unlike* your bank account, however, you will not receive a printed monthly statement. Many crypto investors are fine with keeping their coins in a simple online wallet. There are good reasons, however, to consider more vigorous security.

Even if you opt for an online wallet, it is a good idea to write down your log-in credentials and store them in a safe place. Recently, I received an e-mail from one of my former newsletter subscribers seeking help on a lost crypto wallet. To make a long story short, the wallet contained free cryptocurrency that I'd given to them about five years ago. I responded to the query with the URL of the wallet platform and the support contact details.

While I felt as though this was a reasonable response on my part, the individual sent me an angry follow-up message suggesting it was *my* responsibility to recover their wallet. Note that their wallet was set up independently of me. However, their perception seemed to be that because I was the person who introduced them to cryptocurrency (and gave them some for free), recovering their wallet was my responsibility. I offered several ideas and solutions to help with their predicament, but, ultimately, the matter of wallet recovery will fall on their shoulders to resolve. This story underscores the importance of this section.

You may have heard tales about forgotten bank accounts that were later found through a state 'unclaimed funds' website. I have a relative who had lost track of a $7,000 bank account he'd left behind when he moved from California. This is exactly the kind of thing that regularly happens with cryptocurrency. Unfortunately, there are no 'unclaimed funds' offices for orphaned crypto accounts.

You And *Only* You Are 100% Responsible For Your Log-In Credentials

IT IS YOUR RESPONSIBILITY TO KEEP TRACK OF YOUR CRYPTOCURRENCY. DEPENDING ON HOW

YOU CHOOSE TO STORE IT, LOSING YOUR LOG-IN CREDENTIALS (AND EVEN FORGETTING THE WALLET PLATFORM YOU'RE USING) CAN HAVE VARYING DEGREES OF CONSEQUENCES. An online wallet will typically provide options to reset your log-in (and, in some cases, may also provide a support ticket system). If, on the other hand, you opt for a hardware wallet (more about those in just a bit), you will have no recourse if you lose your log-in and restoration credentials.

Wallet Options

The key to selecting a wallet is to read reviews and select the one that has features compatible with your requirements. A WORD OF WARNING ABOUT WALLET APPS: JUST BECAUSE AN APP IS IN THE APP STORE DOES NOT NECESSARILY MEAN IT IS LEGITIMATE. THERE HAVE BEEN QUITE A FEW SCAMS IN RECENT MONTHS THAT EMPLOYED THE USE OF BOGUS WALLET APPS TO STEAL CRYPTOCURRENCY. The app stores only vet these apps for functionality, and not for their trustworthiness as wallets, apparently.

Most of us that have been around crypto for a while have lost coins due to a wallet scam, or an online wallet provider going out of business. While we are seeing fewer wallet-related scams, it is a good idea to stay with the bigger names and consider dividing your holdings between several wallets as your portfolio grows.

1. Keeping Your Cryptocurrency At An Exchange Or Simple Buying Platform

Pros – Easy To Use

Cons - Higher Hacking Risk

This is what most people do, but it's not without some risk. There are countless stories of online accounts being hacked (some sites have better security than others). The key here is to be sure to avail yourself of all the security measures offered. As mentioned previously, Coinbase (and most exchanges these days) offer two-step authentication. This process requires not just a username and password, but also a *second* randomly-generated password. The secondary log-in can be received by e-mail, the Google authenticator app, or a text sent to your phone.

Consider Using The Coinbase Vault

Coinbase offers an additional layer of protection by providing to customers the option of moving their cryptocurrency to a so-called 'account vault.' Crypto moved to your vault can only be accessed after a two-day waiting period, known as a 48-hour 'thaw.' This added layer of protection makes a lot of sense for those with larger balances.

Each exchange and buying platform will have different security protocols, and you can decide how much or how little security you want in place. ONE OF THE MAJOR DRAWBACKS OF KEEPING YOUR CRYPTO IN AN ONLINE WALLET IS THE RISK OF AN ENTIRE EXCHANGE BEING HACKED. IT HAS HAPPENED. EVEN IF YOU HAVE EMPLOYED SEVERAL LAYERS OF SECURITY WITHIN YOUR OWN INDIVIDUAL ACCOUNT, YOU ARE STILL AT RISK OF A SITE-WIDE SECURITY FAILURE.

Considerations And Precautions When Using Two-Step Authentication

Although it's easier to go with a text message as your second step of authentication, there is a particular risk you should be aware of. A NEW TREND IN HACKING CONCERNS GAINING ACCESS TO THE SECOND STEP OF AUTHENTICATION BY STEALING PHONE NUMBERS. THESE ARE CALLED 'PHONE PORTING' ATTACKS, AND THEY'RE BECOMING INCREASINGLY COMMON. It is for this reason that many people now opt to use the Google Authenticator app for the second authentication step.

Of course, one risk *here* pertains to the potential loss or theft of your mobile phone. This is why you must take the security of your smart phone very seriously. In my own case, without my secret PIN or my thumbprint, my phone will not unlock. The Google authenticator app provides several one-time use backup log-in passwords. These emergency passwords are important should you need to move your account to a new mobile device.

Some online exchanges will allow you to operate with just one level of security, but, in today's world, that would be an enormous hazard. If you don't avail yourself of several layers of security, it is highly unlikely you will garner any sympathy or stand any chance of reimbursement if your account is compromised.

I want to emphasize again that a cryptocurrency account is not at all like a bank or credit card account. MOST OF US ARE COMPLACENT ABOUT ACCOUNT SECURITY BECAUSE WE KNOW THAT THERE ARE LEGAL PROVISIONS TO RESTORE OUR FUNDS IF WE ARE HACKED. HOWEVER, STATE AND FEDERAL LAWS THAT PROTECT BANK AND CREDIT CARD ACCOUNTS DO NOT APPLY TO CRYPTOCURRENCY.

A thief must have your primary password for your secondary password to be of any value. This may require an "Oceans 11" level of thievery, but don't think it can't happen. When a crook has the chance to get their hands on thousands of dollars, they will go to great efforts to do so.

2. Desktop Wallets

Pros - Less Susceptible To Hacking

Cons - More Complicated Than A Simple Online Wallet Or Account

Most cryptocurrency developers make available free software that can be used to store their cryptocurrency on a desktop or laptop. The primary function of this software is to hold your public and private keys (although many also have a mining function, as well).

Using the developer's software is a more complex process than that which is involved with a simple online wallet. For starters, the software will have to sync with the entire blockchain of that currency, and continue to sync with future transactions. There *are* ways to simplify syncing by connecting to a network (node) that has the blockchain already stored on it, but we won't be getting into that here.

Another downside to relying on the developer's software to store crypto is that if your computer is damaged and you have not saved your private keys, your coins can end up being completely lost. There is no one to call, and no 'forgot my password' button to click on. Remember, you have chosen to move your currency to your own computer, and due to the decentralized nature of cryptocurrency, your coins can be lost just like physical money. I READ AN ARTICLE RECENTLY ABOUT TENS OF MILLIONS OF DOLLARS OF BITCOIN LOST WHEN AN OLDER COMPUTER WAS THROWN AWAY. THE OWNER FORGOT THAT THEY HAD STORED HUNDREDS OF BITCOINS ON THE HARD DRIVE. NO KIDDING; WITHOUT THE PRIVATE KEY, MILLIONS OF DOLLARS OF BITCOIN ARE GONE FOREVER!

I don't want to discourage you from using a desktop wallet. Presently, I have some of my coins stored this way, but you must understand the process of restoring your wallet on another computer if your hard drive is damaged. With the cost of laptops now under $300, buying a new laptop for the sole purpose of holding cryptocurrency is a great idea. Pickup up a new laptop for this purpose makes a lot more sense than storing crypto on an older computer. After you transfer your coins to your laptop, you can disconnect it from the Internet (this is known as 'cold storage') and store it in a secure location.

3. Hardware Wallets

Pros - Very secure, portable, and generally not hackable (since they are not connected to the

Internet while in storage)

Cons - A bit more technical than an online wallet; the user must also preserve a 24-word phrase to restore a lost or damaged hardware wallet

I am a big fan of hardware wallets, and they are surprisingly easy to use. The feedback I have received from readers is that the learning curve is minimal. Hardware wallets look a lot like a thumb drive (although some are a bit larger). The big names in hardware wallets today are Trezor, Ledger Nano S, and KeepKey. A hardware wallet will cost between $100 to $150.

If you are just a beginner, and planning to put $100 or less into cryptocurrency, it won't make much sense for you to invest this much in a hardware wallet. On the other hand, if you end up with $1,000 or more in crypto value, either by making subsequent deposits or through the asset's appreciation, a hardware wallet will begin to make sense.

Examples Below Of The Ledger And KeepKey Wallets

Hardware wallets offer the greatest security, overall, because they are not connected to the Internet while in storage. They're connected to your computer only long enough to send or receive cryptocurrency. After the transfer is complete, it is disconnected from the Internet. Since the hardware wallet has no continuous connection to the Internet, it is impossible to be hacked (unless the operating software was tampered with prior to you receiving the wallet device - more on this later).

Remember, most of the news stories about stolen Bitcoin and hacking concern custodial wallets (online accounts). Many people store hardware wallets in a home safe or even a safe deposit box.

Another creative idea to enhance the security of your assets is to utilize what is called a *diversion safe*. A diversion safe looks to be a regular household item, but it actually contains a secret compartment. This can be a faux book on a bookshelf, a container of household cleaner, or even a mock head of lettuce in the refrigerator. These secret compartments make great hiding places for hardware wallets.

While our tendency is to think about digital currency security exclusively in terms of theft by hacking, crypto thieves are now engaging in physical assaults, armed robberies, and even home invasions to capture valuable crypto assets.

If your hardware wallet is lost, damaged, or simply ends up failing, your coins can still be recovered. When setting up your wallet, you will be provided a 24-word recovery phrase (some older wallets use a 12-word phrase). These recovery words (in the proper order) can be used to restore your account to another hardware wallet. I won't get into that process here, but it is basically as simple as having the recovery words written down in the precise order. If you've done this, you have a solid backup method for recovering your coins.

Another hardware wallet security feature is a PIN code. The PIN is required as a first step to accessing the wallet after it is connected to your computer.

All in all, the hardware wallet is a very nice gadget for the cryptocurrency investor, but using one requires a little more of a learning curve than just leaving your coins in an online account (such as Coinbase).

Something else: No matter what your security measures are (diversion safe, traditional safe, or safe deposit box), be sure to keep your 24-word recovery phrase elsewhere. Even if you have a fireproof safe, you should store your 24-word recovery phrase somewhere other than in your home. Remember, however, that this recovery phrase is the 'key to the kingdom.' Anyone who has it can steal your crypto and move it to their own wallet. Sadly, there are now so many – TOO many - stories about roommates, friends, and even relatives stealing crypto.

Your wallet is only as secure as the measures you take to make it so, and you should be very cautious about who you allow into your circle of trust. I have designated one family member as the person who knows how to access my crypto, as a 'just in case.' In the near future I will be retailing a journal for estate planning purposes – a comprehensive record to leave behind for your heirs with details on crypto accounts and passwords.

Restoring A Hardware Wallet

I can now say, from personal experience, that the hardware wallet restoration process *does work*. Recently, I inadvertently deleted everything on one of my hardware wallets while updating the operating software. My heart sank, and I was in a state of panic for several minutes while I completed the recovery process. One by one, I entered the 24-word recovery phrase. After the last word was input, there it was - my wallet was completely restored! While I certainly did not enjoy the anxiety, going through this gave me greater confidence in the ease and success of the recovery process. HOWEVER, IF I DID NOT HAVE THOSE 24 WORDS WRITTEN DOWN, I WOULD HAVE LOST THE FARM.

Staying Anonymous When Receiving Bitcoin

Most HD (hierarchical deterministic) wallets today have a feature that allows the user to generate a new receiving address for every transaction. Think of these new addresses as you would the 'call forwarding' feature of a telephone. You will still receive your Bitcoin payment as usual, but your public address is not exposed. Some wallets are designed to do this automatically, while others offer it as an option.

It is likely that 'unmasking' technology will keep pace with efforts of users to remain anonymous. Nonetheless, I still recommend taking full advantage of all available privacy and security measures. On that note, if privacy is of *paramount* importance to you, Monero, Zcash, and Dash are coins to which you should give particular consideration. These coins possess unique features related to the preservation of security and anonymity. As a result, they are especially attractive choices for the crypto buyer seeking the highest levels of protection available in a coin.

Where To Buy A Hardware Wallet

A good place to start looking at hardware wallets is Amazon, but you should first decide what currencies you plan to buy. Each wallet will be compatible with only a limited list of coins. For example, as of this writing, Ripple cannot be held on the KeepKey wallet, but Ledger Nano S *is* compatible with KeepKey. Do your research on compatibility before shelling out the hundreds of dollars required to purchase a hardware wallet. This technology is developing rapidly, and hardware wallets are quickly expanding their compatibility. Depending on your holdings, it is conceivable THAT YOU MAY NEED MORE THAN ONE HARDWARE WALLET.

Can Hardware Wallets Be Hacked?

There is recent news of hardware wallets being tampered with and then resold online. A scammer can buy a hardware wallet and 'pre-seed' it, giving them access to your 24-word recovery phrase. Then, after the buyer loads crypto on the wallet, it is immediately stolen. *This is why it is imperative that you buy hardware wallets only from manufacturers or authorized resellers*. If you buy through Amazon, be sure that the seller is the original manufacturer, Amazon itself, or an authorized reseller. Also, as soon as you receive your hardware wallet, inspect the packaging to be certain it has not been opened, and update the operating software (details on how to do this will be available through the manufacturer's website).

4. Software Multi-Coin Wallets

Pros – Free, easy to use, and capable of storing multiple cryptocurrencies

Cons – Although more secure than a simple online wallet (or account), they remain online and are less secure than a hardware wallet

Ending up with a lot of wallets can cause confusion. Most of us already have too many passwords to remember. Wouldn't it be easy if we could keep all our cryptocurrency in just one wallet? We're getting there. One free software wallet that I really like is Jaxx (Jaxx.io). All of the functions can be accessed through its mobile app or desktop software. It holds more than fifty coins and is extremely user-friendly. One other difference is that it uses just a 12-word recovery phrase. Another great feature is its integration with coin-exchanging service ShapeShift. This allows you to buy and sell coins within the wallet (more on Shapeshift in Section 4).

Another free multi-coin wallet to consider is Coinomi (Coinomi.com). It is compatible with more than 120 coins, and is especially popular for accumulating lesser-known alt-coins. Coinomi has a very good reputation within the crypto community.

Other Software Wallets to Consider

Electrum (Bitcoin)
Exodus and Edge (multi-coin options)
Wallet.Bitcoin.com (Bitcoin and Bitcoin cash only)

5. Paper Wallets

Pros- Simple to create
Cons - Simple to lose

A 'paper wallet' is merely a piece of paper that has

both your public and private keys printed on it. This is considered 'cold storage,' as your credentials are never accessible online. You can still check your balance at any time by going to Blockchain.info. With your public and private keys, you can easily move your balance to any number of standard crypto wallets. I have used a paper wallet, and while it is 'low tech,' it works. If you have a safe or safe deposit box, these are good options for storage (remember: the information in your paper wallet is all that is needed for a thief to steal your coins).

Paper Wallet Generators

Bitcoinpaperwallet.org
Bitaddress.org
Walletgenerator.net
Mycelium.com

Closing Thoughts On Wallets

If you are happy with dipping your big toe in the crypto sea and buying Bitcoin, Ethereum, Litecoin, or Bitcoin Cash, you can do all of that at Coinbase. If, on the other hand, you want to buy a wider array of coins, you won't be able to avoid having multiple wallets. I love buying lesser-known cryptos, but keep in mind the extra legwork you'll do to find compatible wallets.

In the very near future, many banks will be offering accounts to hold cryptocurrency. For many crypto enthusiasts who are philosophically opposed to mainstream financial institutions, the idea of using a bank to hold digital currency is sacrilege. Nevertheless, I can foresee many people eventually utilizing crypto bank accounts for the sake of convenience.

Section Four: Buying Cryptocurrency 2.0

Earlier in this book, I laid out a Fast Track plan for you to make your first Bitcoin purchase. We will now take the crypto buying process 'next level,' and explore how to hunt and bag your favorite Bitcoin alternatives, as well as review other ways to buy crypto, including through exchanges.

Simple Apps And Platforms For Buying Cryptocurrency

Listed below are the major *non-exchange* crypto-buying platforms. If you simply want to buy and hold one of the major coins, these user-friendly options may be all you need.

Coinbase
CoinMama
Square Cash
Uphold
BitPanda
Robinhood

Buying At A Bitcoin ATM

There are now thousands of Bitcoin ATMs worldwide, and if you live near one, this may be the best option to acquire your initial stake in crypto. I have never personally used one, but there are countless videos online demonstrating how they work. In a nutshell, you insert cash and receive Bitcoin in return. Note that you will need a Bitcoin wallet to actually receive your Bitcoin, so be sure to set that up in advance.

Bitcoin ATM At Grapevine Mills Mall In Dallas

Local Bitcoins

You can also buy Bitcoin from individuals. LocalBitcoins.com has historically been a very popular website to find people selling Bitcoin in your local community. A WORD OF WARNING: THE GOVERNMENT IS AGGRESSIVELY PROSECUTING BITCOIN SELLERS THAT ARE NOT LICENSED AS MONEY TRANSMITTERS (MORE ABOUT THIS LATER). The LocalBitcoins.com site remains quite active, and it appears any potential legal risk associated with the direct, person-to-person Bitcoin sales process rests chiefly with the seller. NEVERTHLESS, CONSULT WITH YOUR OWN ATTORNEY PRIOR TO BECOMING ACTIVE AS A BUYER OR SELLER USING THIS SITE.

Getting Started At Coinbase

As mentioned earlier, the first step in setting up a Coinbase account is identity verification. The reason the identity verification can be challenging is that many of these sites are experiencing unprecedented traffic. Recently, Coinbase was opening more than 100,000 new accounts per week! Just a couple of years back, the process was so much easier. Now, new account-opening procedures are required due to anti-money laundering laws. Crypto trading accounts previously required no identity verification, and, for all practical purposes, were totally anonymous.

While each service will have its own unique requirements for opening an account, *common* requirements include scanning in a driver's license or passport and Social Security number. That doesn't sound so bad, does it? I wish I could tell you it was easy, but I hear back from so many people that what should otherwise be a very simple process can be rather challenging.

A regular source of the trouble is that the ID verification software is not functioning properly. Whether it is a flaw in the software itself or a failure due to system overload, there can be a lot of bumps in the road on the way to opening an account. Most of my accounts were set up long before the huge stampede of new customers, so I can't personally attest to having had these same challenges.

Next, you will have to link your cryptocurrency account to your bank account, so you can fund transactions. Unfortunately, this linking process can *also* prove a challenge while cryptocurrency operations remain in a state of relative infancy.

Still, as frustrating as all of this can be, it's very much worth the trouble, in my opinion. As I say in my online class, once cryptocurrency becomes easy to buy, there will be many *more* buyers, and more buyers will mean higher prices.

LOOK AT YOURSELF AS A PIONEER, AS SOMEONE WHO IS WILLING TO GO WHERE THE ROADS ARE

NOT YET PAVED. REMEMBER THAT DESPITE THE SOMETIMES CHALLENGING VERIFICATION PROCESS, YOU HAVE THE ABILITY RIGHT NOW TO BUY SEVERAL EXCITING CRYPTOS AT BARGAIN PRICES.

Understanding Cryptocurrency Trading Symbols

Similar to stocks, most cryptos have trading symbols that serve as an abbreviation of the full name (for example, Bitcoin's symbol is BTC). If you do decide to trade on an exchange, it is expected that you know the crypto symbol. These abbreviations are readily available, and be sure you have the correct symbol before pulling the trigger on your purchase.

The Differences Between A Simple Buying/Selling Platform And A Cryptocurrency Exchange

There are significant differences between a very simple crypto platform, such as Coinbase, and a full-fledged cryptocurrency exchange. Major exchanges include GDAX (same ownership as Coinbase), Binance, Coinsquare (Canadian-based), Kraken, Poloniex, Gemini (founded by the Winkelvoss twins), Bitfinex, and Bittrex. There are new exchanges popping up all the time, so this is by no means a complete list.

It is important to do your own research before deciding on an exchange, as they have been known to suddenly go out of business and disappear. The largest such debacle involved MT. Gox. It was, at one time, the largest Bitcoin exchange in the world, accounting for 70 percent of all transactions worldwide. The Japan-based exchange suddenly closed in 2014, and later filed for bankruptcy. This development proved to be an earthquake within the fledgling Bitcoin community.

Doing research on an exchange is important, and not difficult. One of the big considerations for many folks is the geographic location of the exchange. Some people prefer a U.S.-based exchange, while others opt for one that is situated offshore.

As you might imagine, going outside the U.S. to find an exchange is popular due to three letters: I-R-S. While I have no reason to believe that cryptocurrency investors, as a whole, are inclined to tax evasion, the recent mass subpoena of Coinbase account records by the IRS has understandably caused a great deal of anxiety in the crypto community. Because of this, offshore exchanges are gaining in popularity.

KEEPING YOUR CRYPTO OFFSHORE IS NO GUARANTEE THAT THE IRS WON'T STILL COME

AFTER YOU. MOST MODERN COUNTRIES HAVE RECIPROCAL AGREEMENTS TO SHARE FINANCIAL INFORMATION WITH THE UNITED STATES. ALSO, ONCE YOU REPATRIATE YOUR CRYPTO AND SPEND IT, YOU WILL HAVE TO EXPLAIN THE SOURCE OF THIS INCOME. BOTTOM LINE: OBEY ALL APPLICABLE LAWS AND PAY YOUR TAXES.

Exchanges offer many more features than simple buying and selling services. You may have access to a margin account (the ability to borrow money to leverage your positions), the option of buying crypto with other crypto, and the ability to use buy and sell limit orders, as is commonly done with stocks.

Be forewarned that many exchanges do not accept fiat currency (such as the U.S dollar) as a means of payment. This means you will need to fund your account with cryptocurrency. In my own case, I buy Bitcoin at Coinbase and transfer it to my exchange account. The Bitcoin I deposit will serve as my base currency to buy other cryptos. For example, if I want to purchase Ethereum by using Bitcoin, I would be trading the BTC/ETH pair. Bitcoin is the most paired crypto on the exchanges, which is why it is your best option for initial account funding at places where fiat currency is not accepted.

A Major Wave Of Crypto Securities Are Coming

There is a large stable of cryptocurrency funds awaiting SEC approval. The most notable of those in the current pipeline is the fund of the Winkelvoss twins - Cameron and Tyler. You may remember their portrayal in the movie *The Social Network*. They were students at Harvard with Facebook founder Mark Zuckerberg. Later, the twins sued Zuckerberg, claiming to have collaborated with him on the creation of Facebook. Eventually, the brothers settled the suit for a reported $65 million.

The Winkelvoss twins (humorously referred to as 'Winkelvi') are true leaders in bringing cryptocurrency to the securities markets. As founders of the Gemini Exchange in 2015, they have worked closely with regulators in the effort to see crypto accepted within traditional financial markets.

Recent news suggests that the SEC is softening its resistance to these crypto funds. With the growing availability of cryptocurrency futures, the approval of crypto funds seems inevitable. Once this happens, it will create an enormous surge of buying. With a limited supply and exploding demand, the future could not be brighter for crypto investors, presently.

How To Buy 'Alt-Coins'

The term 'alt-coin' is short for 'alternative coin,' and generally refers to any coin *other* than Bitcoin. However, the term is more commonly used to reference smaller coins not among the top five or six biggest players in the digital currency space (currently Bitcoin, Bitcoin Cash, Ethereum, Ripple, EOS, and Litecoin). After you make your first purchases of the major coins, you will likely have an interest in next searching among the available alt-coins.

Your curiosity about a particular alt-coin will probably be piqued after you read an article or forum post about it. From there, do a Google search for the name of the coin, and sift through the results to find the official page of the developer. This page will typically provide a brief history of the coin, a link to its desktop wallet, maybe a white paper, and then a list of exchanges where the coin can be purchased. Easy, right? Well, sometimes it is, and sometimes it isn't.

I have run into an array of challenges trying to add an obscure coin to my portfolio. For example, the coin may be available only from a single exchange that does not accept U.S. accounts, or perhaps the exchange it trades on has an impossible verification process. I have even encountered situations where a coin I want is not available on *any* exchange! In that case, the only way to buy it was to go to the forums and find someone willing to sell to me directly.

As bad as all of that may sound, I *do* have good news. There are a couple of tools now available that can make purchasing an alt-coin much easier.

Easy Methods For Buying Alt-Coins

ShapeShift (ShapeShift.io)

ShapeShift is an exchange, of sorts, but it's really a coin conversion service. I have been using it for a few months now, and it is a terrific innovation for buying alt-coins.

Let's say that you'd like to buy Coin X, but you don't want the hassle of opening another account and going through verification. You can easily exchange a coin you own (or a portion of it) for a coin you want to buy. The most common exchange is Bitcoin. The platform has more than sixty coins available for conversion, presently. Opening an account at ShapeShift is not required.

Start by selecting your base currency (the currency you'll be using to fund the transaction) and then select the coin you want to buy. Let's consider an example.

Imagine you have $1,000 worth of Monero and you want to pick up $100 worth of Ethereum. You could easily accomplish this by exchanging a portion of your Monero for the Ethereum (see screenshot below).

Simply follow the indicated steps and plug in the required information, and you will receive your shiny new coin. There are numerous video tutorials on YouTube about how to do this (search for 'How to Use ShapeShift'). I've never had any problems with the platform and have used it countless times.

Still, if you're brand new to ShapeShift, I suggest testing the waters by completing a couple of smaller transactions first. Once you feel that you have a grasp on the process, you can move full steam ahead. Also, don't panic if it takes a few minutes (or occasionally an hour or two) for your order to be completed – that's not uncommon.

Also, be sure to include your refund address (your own 'wallet receive' address) in case the transaction does not go through (see below).

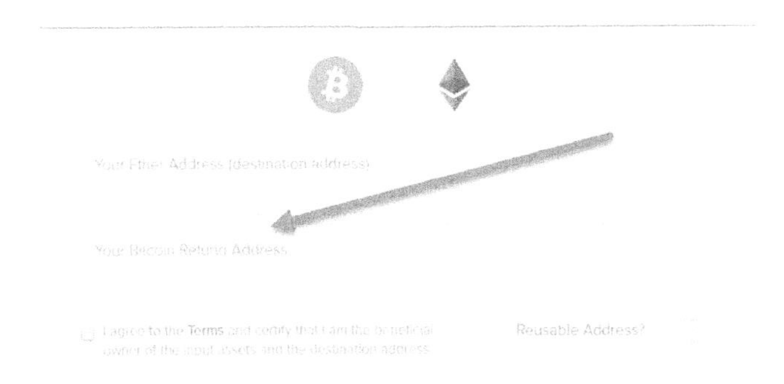

One popular alternative to Shapeshift is Changelly (Changelly.com), another coin exchange service that works similarly to ShapeShift.

ShapeShift Wallet Integration

As mentioned earlier, the Jaxx wallet is fully integrated with ShapeShift, allowing exchanges directly within the wallet. The KeepKey hardware wallet also has the same integration. Keep in mind, however, that you can only use Shapeshift within one of these wallets if that wallet is compatible with the crypto you are converting to.

REMEMBER, NOT ALL WALLETS HOLD ALL COINS.

What Are The Tax Consequences Of Cryptocurrency?

The IRS ruled in 2014 that cryptocurrency is treated as property for tax purposes. It seems as though it would be simple enough to treat your Bitcoin and other cryptos as if they are stocks for tax purposes, right? Well, while the manner in which you would report gains is basically the same, the practical features of crypto investment don't always make it easy to get the information you need for reporting purposes.

For example, crypto investors do not presently receive end-of-year tax reports, summarizing their buy-and-sell activity during the preceding year, the way stock investors receive a Form 1099-B.

An additional wrinkle is that the owner of cryptocurrency must report their profits in U.S. dollars. If you purchased coins using another currency (be it crypto or fiat) you will have to convert your tax basis and capital gain back to U.S. dollars. Further complicating things is the fact that each time you spend crypto, it is considered a sale. Let's say you buy your morning coffee with Bitcoin at a local crypto-friendly cafe. That daily coffee purchase is considered a 'sale,' and must be accounted for as a capital gain or loss.

Tax Preparers Don't Want To Touch Crypto With A Ten-Foot Pole

ONE OF MY READERS ATTEMPTED TO DECLARE A $4,000 CRYPTO GAIN ON HIS TAX RETURN THIS YEAR. HIS TAX PREPARER ADVISED HIM TO WAIT AND "DEAL WITH IT DOWN THE ROAD." THE PREPARER EXPLAINED THAT THE RULES ARE TOO CONFUSING AND THAT NO ONE IS DECLARING THEIR GAINS UNTIL THE THINGS CAN BE MORE CLEARLY UNDERSTOOD.

This might explain the recent IRS announcement that *fewer than 100* crypto investors had declared cryptocurrency gains on their 2017 returns. My simple advice here is to pay your taxes; the IRS is not offering grace to crypto investors.

My guess is that this issue has been given such little attention by lawmakers because so many people expected crypto to be dead by now. The tide of opinion is shifting, however, and perhaps the "powers that be" will give more thought to coming up with sensible, effective rules and systems by which cryptocurrency investors can meet their tax obligations. For example, there could be exemptions for small transactions (like the coffee purchase made with crypto), as well as a capital gains exemption on the first $2,500 per year. There should also be uniform reporting requirements so that crypto investors receive end-of-year tax statements.

Of course, not all crypto investors are anarchists, but animus on their part toward big brother is understandable, given the level of harassment crypto investors have often experienced at the hands of government agencies. Government officials will frequently issue 'warnings' about crypto, suggesting the whole sector is a scam. Unsurprisingly, these declarations often trigger massive sell-offs. Next thing you know, these same government officials have decided crypto is *not* a scam, after all, and has enough legitimacy to be taxed. From there, they say crypto is a security, and subject to the same tax reporting requirements applied to stocks and bonds. Then, after all that, these same feds fail to provide any taxpayer-friendly means by which taxes on crypto can be paid. Government indecisiveness has not only been confusing, but outright maddening for those trying to play by the rules.

Can I Buy Cryptocurrency On Behalf Friends And Relatives?

Once you become the crypto expert within your community, you will no doubt receive requests to make purchases on behalf of others. There are so many reasons why this is a *bad idea*.

Recently, I was visiting some out-of-state friends and the topic of Bitcoin came up. NEXT THING I KNEW, SEVERAL OF THESE GOOD FOLKS HAD THEIR CHECKBOOKS OUT AND REQUESTING THAT I BUY BITCOIN FOR THEM. I HAD TO EXPLAIN THERE WAS NO WAY I COULD DO THAT.

Why You Should Never Be A Straw Crypto Buyer

First, cryptocurrency is subject to capital gains taxes (even if there's not yet a user-friendly way to calculate those). Any crypto account associated with your Social Security number will represent a potential tax liability to you.

Secondly, now that crypto is largely classified as a security, you risk being charged with selling investments without a securities license. Finally (and this one will put you in jail), you may be charged with operating as an unlicensed money transmitter, or perhaps even charged with *money laundering*.

I fear that many people will dismiss my warning here, which is why I'm sharing the story of Jason Klein.

Jason Klein is described in a March 1, 2018 TIME magazine article as a family man "making a little money on the side" buying Bitcoin on behalf of some nice folks he met at a local coffee shop in the Ozarks. Mr. Klein did not realize, however, that the two men he was helping were actually undercover federal agents. Facing a six-figure legal bill and ten years or more in prison, Klein agreed to a plea bargain of 13 months in prison.

Especially shocking is that the total amount of Bitcoin sold to the undercover agents was less than $30,000 - Klein earned just $2,122 in fees for his services. Now he's a convicted felon, going off to prison for a year and a month. CONSIDER YOURSELF WARNED.

Section Five: What Type Of Cryptocurrency Investor Will You Be?

Are You A Hodlr?

'Hodl' is a funny meme that originated from a misspelling of the word 'hold' in one of the online forums. Those that buy cryptocurrency with the intention of holding it for the long term are now called *hodlers.* If you regularly follow crypto news, you will frequently run across the terms 'HODL' and 'hodler,' as they have now become part of the lexicon.

In this section, we will explore a variety of cryptocurrency investing styles. Just as with traditional investing, your approach will be based on your personality, risk tolerance, and available time for managing your holdings.

Buy And Hold

As with stocks, buy and hold is probably the wisest approach to take when investing in cryptocurrency. A while back, a relative asked me how to buy Bitcoin. After several months had passed, I learned they'd bought 10 Bitcoins for $2,000 each. Not even a year later (December 2017) their purchase was worth $200,000 – a

$180,000 profit! They were not trading their account or using any complex strategy; they were just buying and holding. This is likely the smartest approach to crypto investing for most people – invest in one to three major cryptocurrencies, and then forget about them.

Short-Term Trading

Due to the wild swings in the price of cryptocurrency, there is a ripe opportunity for short-term trading, even *day* trading. However, frequent trading comes with greater tax implications. HODLERS BENEFIT FROM BEING TAXED AT A LOW 15% LONG-TERM CAPITAL GAINS RATE (IF THEY MAINTAIN THEIR POSITION FOR MORE THAN ONE YEAR). ON THE OTHER HAND, GAINS REALIZED IN LESS THAN TWELVE MONTHS ARE TAXED AS REGULAR INCOME. THIS CAN MEAN PAYING ALMOST TRIPLE IN TAXES, DEPENDING ON YOUR MARGINAL TAX BRACKET. THIS IS WHY THE BEST PLACE TO TRADE CRYPTO, IF THAT'S WHAT YOU WANT TO DO, IS WITHIN AN IRA (MORE ON BITCOIN IRAS LATER).

The Truth Is That Most People Lose Money On Short-Term Trading

Another downside to active trading is that most people are just not good at it. I worked for many years as a portfolio manager, directing millions of dollars in the investment markets. After years of experience, trading is now second nature to me. However, most people simply do not have the training or time to be profitable short-term traders. Not long ago, I read an article that confirmed 95 percent of those who trade the stock market underperform a simple S&P 500 index fund. While the crypto markets are different from the stock market in many ways, the comparison between the two in this context is reasonable.

Trading Tools

If you are going to actively trade the crypto markets, you should choose a research approach for making buy and sell decisions. In stock market investing, there are two principal research approaches: *fundamental analysis* and *technical analysis*. These two, time-honored methods of evaluating investments are applicable to cryptocurrency, as well.

Fundamental analysis in the world of stocks is focused on a company's earnings, prospects for future growth, and other similar evaluations. Technical analysis, on the other hand, is exclusively concerned with examining the historical price action of an investment as a means to predicting its *future* price action. Technical analysis can be helpful to crypto investors who wish to trade more actively.

Technical analysis relies on the use of charts and graphs to draw a picture of an investment's price action. As noted in the previous paragraph, the basis of technical analysis is the idea that the historical performance of an asset is a reliable indicator of future performance. That is a simple description, however, and there is much more to learning, and effectively applying, technical analysis.

If you are short-term trading, you should pay particular attention to the trend lines associated with the price movements of the crypto you're watching. Note that a trend line is *not* the graphical display of a crypto's price action. A trend line is a straight line that is added to the chart to help clarify how the price of a crypto is trending, overall. For example, a trend line will often be used to connect the higher highs a crypto is achieving to show that its overall trend is up, or, conversely, to connect its lower lows to illustrate it is broadly declining in price.

NOTE: THE PREVIOUS PARAGRAPH IS A VASTLY SIMPLISTIC DESCRIPTION OF TREND LINE ANALYSIS. However, an in-depth discussion of technical analysis falls outside the scope of this book. If you want to learn more about technical analysis, a great Google search phrase is "technical analysis for beginners," from which you'll find a variety of excellent online resources, many of them available for free.

As for physical books on the subject, one of the very best remains *Technical Analysis of the Financial Markets* by John J. Murphy. Although last updated about 20 years ago, it remains the standard for manuals on technical analysis. If you would prefer to start with an easier read on the topic, *Technical Analysis for Dummies* by Barbara Rockefeller is very good (and ignore the title; even those well-versed in technical analysis can derive value from the book).

A Candlestick Chart of Bitcoin's Price Action That Includes an Overlay of the Popular 50-Day Moving Average Indicator

One excellent site used by many traders to actually perform technical analysis on crypto price movements is TradingView.com. TradingView.com offers both free and paid membership levels, and you'll find there all of the technical analysis tools you would ever want. I especially like the discussion groups, where users share their own trading tips and strategies. If you are new to crypto trading, you can get some great insight from other traders in the discussion groups.

Sentiment Analysis - The Best Trading Tool Of All?

ONE EXTREMELY VALUABLE TRADING TOOL THAT MOST CRYPTO INVESTORS ARE *NOT* USING IS SENTIMENT ANALYSIS. SENTIMENT ANALYSIS, OR HOW TRADERS FEEL ABOUT A GIVEN CRYPTOCURRENCY, MAY BE THE MOST ACCURATE PREDICTOR OF PRICE MOVEMENT.

The free analytics tool Google Trends can be very helpful in performing sentiment analysis. When you punch in a given search term at Google Trends, a graph will be returned that illustrates the current popularity of that term. For example, should you determine that there are increases in searches for 'Bitcoin,' you would consider that to be a positive development for the entire sector (in the way a rising tide lifts all boats). A more helpful application of Google Trends is using it to gauge the search frequency of specific coins; the more people there are searching for information on a coin, the more buyers there will be.

Another great site available to help you with sentiment analysis is Crypto-Sentiment.com. You can receive their free weekly sentiment reports by participating in their surveys.

Bottom-Fishers

YOU ARE TOO SMART TO PAY THOUSANDS OF DOLLARS FOR A SINGLE BITCOIN, RIGHT? INSTEAD, YOU ARE GOING TO DISCOVER THE BITCOIN OF TOMORROW AND BUY IT TODAY FOR JUST A FEW CENTS. NO SARCASM INTENDED HERE; THIS CAN BE A TERRIFIC IDEA.

I will confess that I'm always on the hunt for the next Bitcoin. That is the reason why I presently own almost 50 different cryptocurrencies, many of which are worth less than a dollar (cryptos under a dollar are often called 'penny cryptos'). I combine this shotgun approach with another strategy I call 'profit rolling.' The idea is to take a portion of my windfalls and roll it into penny cryptos. I consider it betting with the house's money. Although I don't like to use the analogy of gambling within the context of investing, I think it fits in this particular context. I HAVE OFTEN JOKED THAT BUYING PENNY CRYPTOS IS A LOTTERY FOR SMART PEOPLE. DON'T WE ALL WANT TO BE THAT

GUY WHO PUT $100 IN BITCOIN IN 2010 AND ENDED UP WITH A $250 MILLION-DOLLAR FORTUNE? Because of both the risk and potential reward of penny cryptos, it makes sense to start out with an initial investment of $25 or less.

I will admit that managing a portfolio of nearly 50 cryptos is a lot of work. For starters, I had to go through a great deal of trouble to buy many of these coins, since they don't trade on the major crypto exchanges or ShapeShift. I also had to find wallets that would hold these dark-horse picks. However, I am convinced that some of these are going to really pay off in the coming months.

Finding Penny Cryptos Using CoinMarketCap

ONE INTERESTING EXERCISE IS TO CLICK TWICE ON THE PRICE COLUMN AT COINMARKETCAP.COM AND REVIEW THE RANKING OF THE TOP 100 COINS BY LOWEST TO HIGHEST PRICE. These lowest price coins in the top 100 cryptos are longshots with enormous potential return. Most of these coins cost just a few cents, and some are less than a penny. All a bottom-fisher needs is for one of these penny cryptos to catch fire. Take for example, Kin, which is the lowest price coin in the top 100 today (see graphic below), trading for .000222. With $50 I can buy over 200,000 units of this coin!

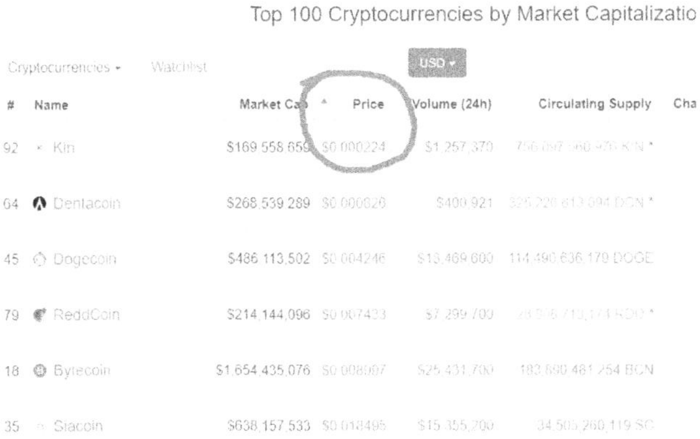

Top 100 Cryptocurrencies by Market Capitalizatio

Cryptocurrencies ▾ Watchlist USD ▾

#	Name	Market Cap	Price	Volume (24h)	Circulating Supply
92	Kin	$169,558,659	$0.000224	$1,257,370	756,097,560,976 KIN *
64	Dentacoin	$268,539,289	$0.000826	$400,921	325,226,613,094 DCN *
45	Dogecoin	$486,113,502	$0.004246	$13,469,600	114,490,636,179 DOGE
79	ReddCoin	$214,144,096	$0.007433	$7,299,700	[illegible] RDD *
18	Bytecoin	$1,654,435,076	$0.008997	$25,431,700	183,890,481,254 BCN
35	Siacoin	$638,157,533	$0.018495	$15,355,200	34,505,260,119 SC

Dollar Cost Averaging

A shrewd way to initially enter the cryptocurrency market is by averaging yourself in. *Dollar cost averaging* has long been a popular approach among stock and mutual fund investors, and it works just as well for crypto investing. The idea is that it is wiser to make regular, ongoing investments than to invest a great deal of money in a single lump sum and risk buying at the top. Dollar cost averaging is customarily done on a monthly basis, but other intervals, like quarterly, can work, too - just select a time frame that makes sense and begin your systematic investing.

I used a form of dollar cost averaging when I was professionally managing investments for clients. In that case, I would typically move a new client into the market in thirds over a three-month period. This was especially appropriate when dealing with larger sums, but even if you plan to start purchasing crypto with a modest amount, you may still want to consider 'averaging in.'

Resist the temptation to jump in all at ounce for *fear of missing out* (FOMO). FOMO is an emotional response by some investors to frothy markets, where they rush in and invest their available investment on day one. You may have to wait months to get your head back above water if you buy at a peak.

Because I want to keep things simple, I won't go any further with the subject of investing strategies. Suffice it to say, if you believe that Bitcoin and your other favorite cryptos are going to be a lot higher a year from now, you don't want to get too bogged down trying to time your entry into the market. However, if you're uncertain about just how strong the performance might be in the near term, a more measured approach to investing in cryptos can be a great idea.

Why Is Cryptocurrency, Including Bitcoin, So Volatile?

The wild price swings of Bitcoin and other cryptos can be maddening. To make matters worse, you never get a break, as these are 24/7 markets. Unlike your stock portfolio that at least gives you nights and weekends off from the emotional roller coaster, you don't get a reprieve from your crypto holdings. With the availability of mobile apps like CoinMarketCap, real-time prices stream day and night. In fact, some of my readers have told me they awaken several times each night to check the value of their portfolios (I sometimes do this myself).

There are a couple of reasons why the crypto markets are so volatile. First, these are not mature markets. It took decades of fine tuning to reach the point of so-called efficient and orderly markets on Wall Street. Crypto remains very much in its infancy, and even the largest crypto exchanges have been in existence for less than three years.

The second reason for the volatility may resonate more with those of you who already closely follow crypto market news. This is a highly emotional market. Time and again, investors *overreact* to news and events. As a result, good news tends to cause too much of a bump, and bad news almost always prompts sensational drops. And the fact these markets are still so young will often exaggerate the reactions.

Many who've invested in crypto more recently have done so based largely on the sudden popularity and fad of cryptocurrency. TABLOID-

DRIVEN BUYERS TEND TO PURCHASE BASED ON HYSTERIA. THEY BUY AFTER READING AN ARTICLE ABOUT A 20-SOMETHING BITCOIN MILLIONAIRE AND SELL WHEN THEY SEE 'THE DEATH OF BITCOIN' ON THE COVER OF A MAGAZINE AT THEIR LOCAL BOOKSTORE. I WOULD GUESS THAT AS MUCH AS ONE-THIRD OF THE CRYPTO MARKETS ARE COMPOSED OF VOLATILE PLAYERS. KATY BAR THE DOOR IF KIM KARDASHIAN EVER TWEETS SOMETHING NEGATIVE ABOUT BITCOIN!

Section Six: Following The Action

Depending on how much money you plan to invest, and how much available time you have, you will need to come up with a plan to stay on top of the lightning-fast world of cryptocurrency. It can be a real challenge tracing the latest news and developments on more than 1,500 coins and tokens in the market.

Already, it seems as though everyone's brother-in-law now has an online course, book, or seminar on crypto (including yours truly at BitcoinBloodhound.com). One temptation for new investors is to buy every program they can get their hands on (I did that myself). I thought by signing up for multiple courses, I would gain some new perspectives and ideas for this book. The truth is that my expenditures largely proved to be wasted money.

Beware Of Crypto Clickbait

The following type of e-mail offer is very common nowadays: "What three-cent crypto is going to $100 this year? Just click here and get the free e-mail report." The next thing you know, you've been sucked into a marketing funnel from which you can't escape. In my experience, courses that use these kinds of hooks are usually overpriced and of little value.

If you do opt to take an online class, focus on those that offer practical, easy-to-execute strategies. One the main features of my own course is a private Facebook group. This group is very active, with relevant discussions and ideas that can be applied immediately. Although I am officially the moderator, I see myself as a student along with the other members of the group. It is a forum of mutual respect, healthy debate, and a robust sharing of ideas (and I learn as much from my students as they learn from me).

The world of cryptocurrency is advancing so rapidly that everyone needs a plan to stay informed. Because my member forum is a private group, it is much more like a meet-up of friends. You won't experience the same frenzy you'll encounter at Reddit and other public groups. Public forums have their place, but they can get a little noisy, and many are nothing more than platforms for debate. Participate in forums that keep you informed and provide an ongoing source of actionable ideas (like over at Reddit). Udemy is another site with several very affordable crypto classes (most for under $20). One of the things I especially like about Udemy is that you can view a video sample of the class before enrolling.

What Are The Best Websites And Publications?

A great way to discover websites and blogs to follow is to do a Google news search for the coins you're watching. You can also set up Google News alerts to receive breaking news on your coins. Over time, you will discover your own favorite list of blogs to follow. To help keep up with the (roughly) 50 blogs I read, I use Feedly. Feedly is a feed reader that displays all the new articles from these blogs in a single-page view. The service costs $5 monthly and is worth much more than that to me because of the massive time savings I enjoy.

My Recommended Short List Of News Sites And Blogs

Bitcoin Magazine
CNBC.com/Bitcoin
Coin Telegraph
Cryptocoin News
Reddit (read discussion groups on the coins you follow)
Bitcoin Talk
Crypto Insider
Bitcoin.com
CoinDesk
CCN.com

The Most Practical Way To Stay Informed And Keep Learning

I visit CoinMarketCap.com more than a dozen times per day. It only takes a minute to become familiar with the layout, and there is also a mobile app. The home page consists of a table that displays the top 100 cryptocurrencies, based on market capitalization. Market capitalization (market cap) is the total market value of a particular crypto, and is determined by multiplying the current price of a coin by the total number of units in circulation.

The market cap figure is helpful because it provides a sense of how widely a coin is being adopted. You can manipulate the columns at CoinMarketCap.com to base the ranking on a variety of measurements. For example, you might want to rank the top 100 coins by profit and loss over the most recent 24-hour period; by price per coin; or even by trading volume. There is also a nice portfolio tracking tool on the mobile app that can be used to monitor the overall value of your crypto portfolio.

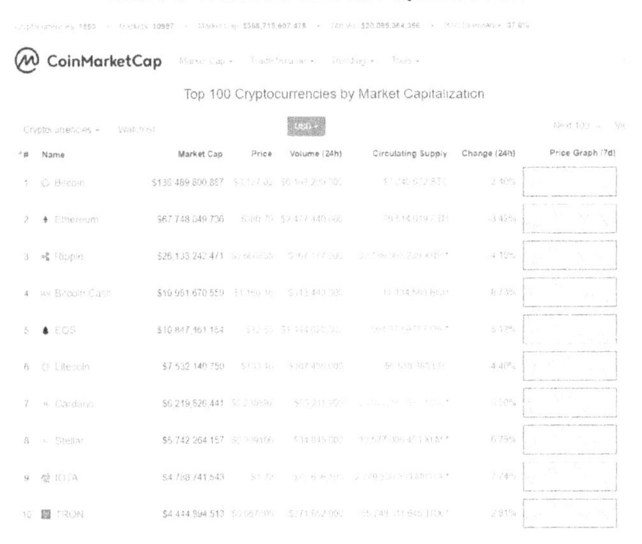

CoinMarketCap

Top 100 Cryptocurrencies by Market Capitalization

#	Name	Market Cap	Price	Volume (24h)	Circulating Supply	Change (24h)	Price Graph (7d)
1	Bitcoin	$136,489,800,887	[illegible]	[illegible]	[illegible]	2.40%	
2	Ethereum	$67,748,049,736	[illegible]	[illegible]	[illegible]	-3.43%	
3	Ripple	$26,133,242,471	[illegible]	[illegible]	[illegible]	-4.10%	
4	Bitcoin Cash	$19,961,670,559	[illegible]	[illegible]	[illegible]	8.73%	
5	EOS	$10,847,461,164	[illegible]	[illegible]	[illegible]	[illegible]	
6	Litecoin	$7,532,140,750	[illegible]	[illegible]	[illegible]	-4.40%	
7	Cardano	$6,219,626,441	[illegible]	[illegible]	[illegible]	[illegible]	
8	Stellar	$5,742,264,157	[illegible]	[illegible]	[illegible]	6.75%	
9	IOTA	$4,788,741,543	[illegible]	[illegible]	[illegible]	7.74%	
10	TRON	$4,444,894,513	[illegible]	[illegible]	[illegible]	2.81%	

Bitcoin.com just launched its own price-tracking tool called Satoshi Pulse. It is not yet available as an app, but it's easy to save the web address to the home screen of your mobile device. It has a little different feel than CoinMarketCap, and I encourage you to check it out (markets.Bitcoin.com).

How To Use The Data At Coinmarketcap.Com

I use the market data at CoinMarketCap.com in several ways. Of course, I follow the price movements of the coins that I own. I also keep an eye out for up-and-comers. For example, if a coin has a spike in trading volume, or a spectacular 24-hour performance, these can be clues to discovering new additions to your portfolio. You'll find that the more you study the top-100 list, the more pieces of information will jump out at you. While a single day's stellar performance is not enough for me to buy a particular coin, it *will* prompt me to put that coin on my radar screen for further research.

Look For Coins That Are Bucking The Trend On A Losing Day

There are days when the entire roster of cryptos is glowing red, indicating losses over the most recent 24 hours. However, despite that broad wave of negative movement, you might see one or two coins that are green, indicating gains over the same period. IT IS WORTH TAKING A CLOSER LOOK AT COINS THAT ARE BUCKING THE TREND AND RISING WHEN ALL OTHERS ARE TANKING. I HAVE UNCOVERED SOME REAL WINNERS USING THIS APPROACH.

Radio Shows And Podcasts

After you dive into the deep end of the crypto pool, you just might end up with an insatiable appetite for all things cryptocurrency. One thing I quickly discovered is that the crypto community is very diverse. It includes financial nerds (like me), high-net-worth professional investors, libertarians, anarchists, preppers, and even secessionists. Don't be dissuaded from your crypto journey if you bump into people with wildly different lifestyles and viewpoints. Speaking as an evangelical Christian, I can tell you that I get more than a little pushback from some of my peers in that community who want to paint everyone in the crypto 'brotherhood' as criminals, money launders, and consumers of online porn.

It should be noted that radio and podcast hosts covering crypto are also investors. While the shows listed below are certainly a tremendous resource, be advised that hosts (including myself) tend to be inherently biased in favor of the coins in their own portfolios.

Jim Paris Live is the name of my own radio show, and it airs Sunday nights from 9 to 11 p.m. ET on the Genesis Communications Network (stream available at TalkStreamLive.com). Although I don't cover cryptocurrency every week, it *is* a frequent topic. You can learn more about my show, including the various options for downloading it, over at JimParisRadio.com.

Free Talk Live is a nightly live radio show based in Keene, New Hampshire (FreeTalkLive.com). Hosted by Ian Freeman and a rotating panel of libertarians, the show frequently focuses on Bitcoin and cryptocurrency. If you don't find it on a local radio station, you can listen online at TalkStreamLive.com from 7 to 10 p.m. ET. As a regular listener, you'll pick up a lot of useful information. I am not a libertarian, and don't necessarily agree with all of their political views, but I find the discussion interesting. Also, *The Crypto Show* (cryptoshow.com) on the Liberty Network is another great resource.

I love podcasts, and recently discovered Listen Notes (ListenNotes.com), a topic-based podcast search engine. Using Listen Notes, you can search for podcasts based on individual episode topics. Input the search phrase 'Bitcoin' or 'cryptocurrency,' and you will find hundreds of podcast episodes you can download for free. Without a tool like Listen Notes, most crypto enthusiasts miss these one-off episodes. Take *The Tim Ferriss Show*, for example. Host Tim Ferriss only occasionally discusses crypto, but when he does, the episodes are of *tremendous* value. By the way, I consider episode #244 of *The Tim Ferriss Show* to be mandatory listening for any crypto enthusiast - it's a two-and-a-half-hour interview with crypto pioneer Nick Szabo.

Leverage your time in the car, at the gym, and working around the house listening to crypto podcasts. If you consistently listen to even just one or two podcasts, you will be up to speed in no time. By the way, my favorite app for downloading and managing podcasts on my smart phone is PocketCasts.

Top Cryptocurrency Podcasts

Unchained Podcast
Invest Like The Best
Tim Ferris (multiple topics including crypto)
The Bitcoin Podcast
The Third Web
Bitcoin Uncensored
Epicenter
Block Zero
Coin Mastery
The Bad Crypto Podcast
Coin Talk
Let's Talk Bitcoin
Crypto Street Podcast
Bitcoins And Gravy
Ledger Cast

YouTube As A Resource

If you are not a regular visitor to YouTube, you might think that it's mostly videos of laughing babies and people jumping off roofs into backyard swimming pools. As much time as I spend online, I have only just recently started tapping into YouTube's vast educational resources. In the private Facebook group that I moderate, I answer many of the questions by simply posting a link to a YouTube video. Common questions with great YouTube answers include:

"How do I send and receive money from my crypto wallet?"
"How can I use ShapeShift to exchange one coin for another?"
"How do I make a purchase using the Binance exchange?"

There's countless more, but you get the picture. YouTube is a terrific 'how-to' resource for budding crypto investors. Also, if you happen to find a few crypto 'voices' that resonate with you, subscribe to their YouTube channels so that you receive notifications when new videos are posted.

Top YouTube Crypto Channels

Data Dash
Crypto Lark
Crypto Daily
Trevon James
Suppoman
Crypto News
Chris Dunn
Ivan On Tech
Bitcoin Official
They Call Me Dan
CryptoSpark
CryptoTips
Crypto Oracle
Coin Mastery
Michael Crypto

Crypto Nick
Box Mining
The Chart Guys
Sunny Decree

Do You Recommend Attending Any Of The Popular Bitcoin And Crypto Conferences?

Once you become a crypto enthusiast yourself, you might consider attending some live events. The conferences are expensive - most are $1,000 or more just for admission, not including lodging or airfare.

One reason *not* to attend (other than the cost) is that many of the conferences later release the audio and video content of the major presentations. Even in cases where that does not happen, the important announcements are widely reported in the crypto media.

If you are like me, and simply want to learn more about the investment aspects of crypto, these events may not have all that much to offer. You would probably be better served by saving the $2,000 to $3,000 (estimated total trip cost) and using the money to buy more crypto. However, if you're seeking a job within the crypto industry, or happen to have a crypto-related business to promote, these conferences can be valuable networking opportunities.

Section Seven: My Own Crypto Hot List

Don't Jump On The ICO (Initial Coin Offerings) Bandwagon

Let me start this section by sharing with you that I have refrained from climbing aboard the ICO 'bandwagon.' There are so many reasons to be wary of Initial Coin Offerings. For starters, the securities regulators are going after them with a renewed vigor. For several years, ICOs were able to skirt the securities laws by operating in what was an unregulated space. However, ICOs are now officially classified as securities, and so raising money to launch an ICO must be done within the framework of the securities laws of the United States or any other country where funds are raised.

I would never completely rule out buying an ICO, but I have not done so yet. If an ICO strikes you as compelling, limit your risk by investing just a small sum – there's nothing wrong with investing tiny amounts (that you're OK with entirely losing) in ICOs in hopes of landing cryptocurrency's version of a winning lottery ticket.

If Not Through An ICO, How Does A Cryptocurrency Initially Get Into Circulation?

There are generally three ways a new cryptocurrency breaks into circulation, other than through an ICO.

One way is by being *spent* into circulation. Those providing services to the developer's network are paid with the currency. The recipient can hold it, sell it on an exchange, or swap it for another cryptocurrency. Another way a currency can be distributed is by way of an incentive for participating in a social network (see information on Steemit in Section 10).

The third and most well-known method by which a cryptocurrency enters circulation is through the process of *mining* (mining is discussed in Section 10).

Listed below are a few of my own cryptocurrency holdings (as of the time this book was written).

The Big Names:

Bitcoin

You have to own the market leader, right? The amount of Bitcoin I own as a percentage of my holdings varies. It almost always represents one of my top two or three positions. I think of it as my 'blue chip' crypto stock. In addition to owning Bitcoin outright, I have exposure to Bitcoin within my IRA through the Grayscale Bitcoin Trust, an exchange-traded note. I believe that every crypto portfolio should have Bitcoin as an anchor position.

Bitcoin Cash

I never got down in the mud and joined the 'Bitcoin versus Bitcoin Cash' debate. I think both sides have good arguments, and there's no disputing that the Bitcoin network had become too slow and too expensive. As a result of the so-called 'hard fork,' I received one free Bitcoin Cash coin for each Bitcoin I owned. I have not, however, joined the movement of enthusiasts that believe Bitcoin Cash is the new Bitcoin. Bitcoin Cash continues to do well, and I plan to hold it for the long term. It may not be a replacement for Bitcoin, but it *is* a solid crypto to have in your portfolio.

What Is The Difference Between Bitcoin And Bitcoin Cash?

Bitcoin had reached the point where it was growing faster than the present network infrastructure could handle. Scaling challenges were resulting in long delays and high transaction fees. A mutiny erupted within the Bitcoin community regarding what to do about these issues. One faction wanted to implement major changes to the Bitcoin network, while the other faction did not agree with this new direction. The bottom line is that since there was no agreement on proposed changes, a group within the Bitcoin community split off and created their own version of the cryptocurrency, calling it Bitcoin Cash. Bitcoin Cash can be purchased at Coinbase, as well as through all of the major exchanges.

When the split (the 'hard fork') took place in August 2017, everyone who owned Bitcoin received an equal amount of Bitcoin Cash.

We won't spend any more time on it here, but for those interested in delving deeper into the history of the Bitcoin vs. Bitcoin Cash issue, do a Google search for SegWit (Segregated Witness) versus Bitcoin Cash.

Ripple XRP

Ripple XRP has been a fascination of mine for several years now. In fact, many in the crypto world consider me a prophet due to my December 2013 YouTube video titled, 'Is Ripple the Next Bitcoin?' Ripple is presently the third-largest cryptocurrency in the world, based on market capitalization. As mentioned earlier, I started buying Ripple for myself and then began giving it away to newsletter subscribers.

One of the big reasons for the enthusiasm surrounding Ripple XRP is the price per coin. Ripple is presently trading for 70 cents. Earlier this year it briefly jumped to a high of $3.65.

Despite being the third-largest crypto, Ripple offers an extremely attractive price point. Granted, the reason the price is this low is because there will be a total of 100 billion coins in circulation (compared to Bitcoin's 21 million). Nonetheless, investors unable to buy a full Bitcoin can't help but be enamored with the idea of getting more than 100 coins for $100. Ripple is attracting a lot of crypto newcomers because of both its affordable price and perceived future viability.

Ripple Is Not Decentralized

Among the most passionate arguments made against Ripple is its 'centralized network.' The main reason that decentralization is such a big issue with crypto enthusiasts is the belief that it establishes privacy and security. However, the degree of privacy and anonymity created through decentralization is subject to some debate. Still, it's hard to disagree with the general consensus that a decentralized network gives more power to the people.

With true peer-to-peer transactions, there's more privacy and security. They also make it harder for asset confiscation to occur. Without so much as a court hearing, the IRS can take your paycheck and your bank account. However, this kind of heavy-handed thuggery is much more difficult for a government to effect when dealing with a decentralized asset like Bitcoin.

Still, it's not as though the government is without any options if it decides it wants your crypto. A federal judge could order you to turn over your holdings, or jail you for contempt. This is exactly what happened to infomercial guru Kevin Trudeau when he refused to surrender overseas assets. He was not a holder of crypto, but the mechanism works the same way. Trudeau was eventually sentenced to ten years in prison.

Crypto Purists Consider Owning Ripple Tantamount To Sleeping With The Enemy

Another aspect of Ripple that is sacrilege to many crypto enthusiasts is its integration into the banking system. This is because the traditional financial marketplace is anathema to the alternative asset community, and particularly to crypto investors and adherents. Accordingly, Ripple's alliance with banks is viewed by many as a case of 'sleeping with the enemy.' WHILE I AM NO FAN OF BANKS MYSELF, I ACCEPT THE REALITY THAT REVOLUTIONS TEND NOT TO HAPPEN OVERNIGHT. IT IS HIGHLY UNLIKELY THAT CRYPTO WILL COMPLETELY REPLACE TRADITIONAL ASSETS, INCLUDING CASH, IN THE NEAR TERM. WHAT IS *MORE* PROBABLE IS A CONTINUED MELDING OF CRYPTOCURRENCY WITH THE BANKING SYSTEM.

Plans are already in motion for the complete integration of crypto into the U.S. banking system. Ripple's tactic of bringing crypto *to* banks may just turn out to be the most brilliant chess move in the history of the crypto movement - those at the foundation of Ripple are gaining institutional support from the very same people working to destroy Bitcoin.

I invest to make money and don't spend a lot of time indulging philosophical debates about how the sausage is made. Many readers may consider it traitorous of me to be giving such a positive review of Ripple, but, as I see it, I'm just covering another number on the roulette wheel. I believe there are a lot of crypto investors who very quietly own Ripple themselves. However, admitting to it publicly might diminish the anarchist 'credentials' some of them value. I CONTINUE TO BELIEVE THAT RIPPLE XRP MAY HAVE THE GREATEST UPSIDE POTENTIAL OF ANY

CRYPTOCURRENCY TODAY.

Ethereum

Ethereum is presently the second-biggest cryptocurrency in the world, based on market cap, and the current favorite to overtake Bitcoin for the top spot. Frequently referred to as Bitcoin 2.0, Ethereum offers many new innovations not available in its predecessor (Bitcoin was launched nearly six years before Ethereum).

Ethereum is not just faster than Bitcoin; it offers a platform for the creation of *tokens*. While both coins and tokens are cryptocurrency, a token represents a unit of value, and is not currency, per se. A token is more like a gift card, whereas a digital coin is actual currency in the same way the dollars in your pocket are (ostensibly) currency.

Coinbase recently announced (as of March 2018) plans to integrate Ethereum tokens into their platform. These are known as 'ERC20' tokens. 'ERC' stands for 'Ethereum Request for Comment,' and refers to the technical means by which so-called 'smart contracts' are implemented within the Ethereum blockchain. The most successful token to date is EOS which, at this writing, is number five in market cap among all cryptos.

Once tokens can be held in a Coinbase wallet, they will explode in popularity. Creating a token is a fairly simple process and can be done for free at several websites (the most popular is MyEtherWallet.com).

Bottom line: Ethereum is another 'must-have' cryptocurrency for the serious investor.

Litecoin

Litecoin launched in 2011, which means it's just a little newer than Bitcoin. Because it has been around for so (relatively) long, it's a popular crypto among Bitcoin's early adopters.

The primary difference between Litecoin and Bitcoin is transaction processing speed. As with Ethereum, Litecoin has a significantly faster platform than Bitcoin. There are also minor differences in the mining process and the programming. It's fair to say, however, that Litecoin is almost identical to Bitcoin (although Litecoin's protocol allows for four times as many coins to be created). Litecoin has historically sat in the top five at CoinMarketCap.com, but was recently knocked down to number six by EOS, the Ethereum token.

THE REASON LITECOIN IS NOT MORE POPULAR IS BECAUSE CRYPTO INVESTORS ARE LOOKING FOR

THE *NEXT GENERATION* OF BITCOIN, NOT A COIN THAT IS NEARLY A CLONE. That said, I still consider it a solid coin to hold due to its early entry into the crypto space.

Lesser-Known Coins On My Radar Screen

CloudCoin

You will not find CloudCoin on the CoinMarketCap top 100 list, nor presently available on any of the exchanges. However, at this writing, you *can* buy CloudCoin for just a nickel. The creator, Sean Worthington, was a recent guest on my radio show (the episode is available on both iTunes and YouTube). Worthington is a college professor and created CloudCoin as the first cloud-based digital currency.

There are several other unique features about CloudCoin that caught my attention. First, there's Worthington's proprietary system, called RAIDA (Redundant Array of Independent Detection Agents), which provides authentication and prevents double spending. Secondly, because it is in the cloud, there is no wallet required - the currency is embedded within a simple .JPG image. There is also built-in theft protection.

If you are interested in learning more about CloudCoin, be sure to listen to the interview I did with Sean Worthington. Because this coin has so many unique features and so few people know about it, I'm convinced there's a lot of upside here. To find out more about CloudCoin and purchase their starter kit, visit Cloudcoin.global. I particularly love the educational package they've been offering for about $12, which includes 386 CloudCoins, an eBook, and their desktop software (Cloudservice.academy).

Other Names To Consider

Many readers have asked me to offer a short list of other coins that I like. While I don't share the entire list of my holdings, here are a few more for consideration. I own some of these coins right now, while I continue to evaluate the others.

Dash
Zcash
Monero
Bitshares
EOS
Steem
Steem Dollar
Ethereum Classic
Monacoin
IOTA
NEM
Cardano
Stellar

Stratis
Quantum
Dogecoin
ZenCash
RavenCoin
Cloudcoin
Verge
Stella Lumens
Tron

What To Look For When Considering A New Coin

Many newbies buy a coin simply because it is going up in value. While there are obviously no guarantees that a crypto investment will work out favorably, take at least a few minutes to do some research ('due diligence') on a coin you're considering to help determine the odds it will work out. Just because a particular coin is rising in value 'in the moment' does not necessarily mean it is a good choice for your portfolio.

Questions To Ask:

What is the purpose of the coin?

What is the track record of the developers behind the coin?

What is the plan for market penetration with the coin?

How widely is the coin accepted (market capitalization)?

What unique features does it have that are not already present in an established coin?

What wallets are available to hold the coin?

How easy (or difficult) is it to buy?

Section Eight: How To Spend Bitcoin And Cryptocurrency

Bitcoin is real money. There is no better way to prove this to yourself and skeptical friends than to buy something with it. You can purchase anything - from a cup of coffee to real estate - with Bitcoin. As a matter of fact, there are several recent examples of homes for sale where the sellers were ONLY ACCEPTING BITCOIN as payment!

A few months back, the topic of Bitcoin came up among a group of my friends. One skeptical buddy of mine said, "Well, let me know when you are able to cash any of that in and do something with it." I smiled and mentioned that just the day before I had sold some of my shares of the Grayscale Bitcoin Trust and bought a trip to Italy and Switzerland. Well, THAT wiped the smirk off his face.

I run into plenty of people who are completely ignorant about Bitcoin, but yet they never miss a chance to take potshots at it. The laughs quickly stop, however, when I show them a new laptop, a smart phone, airline tickets, or a dream trip to Europe...ALL PAID FOR WITH BITCOIN.

Purse.io

Purse.io is a specialized crypto merchant service that enables you to grab discounts of up to 33 percent on Amazon as long as you pay with Bitcoin. A more typical savings is around 15 percent, but up to 33 percent is certainly possible. In recent months, I have purchased a tablet computer, a high-end digital camera, an expensive camera lens, and a drone using Purse.io, and I saved $180 (an average of about 10 percent overall). As a matter of fact, if I was not in a hurry to receive these items, I could have selected a higher discount option (the larger the discount you choose, the longer it will take for your order to be matched). Items ship directly from Amazon, and Bitcoin payments are held in escrow until the buyer confirms delivery.

Note that it is *not* Amazon providing the discount. The framework of the process involves a large pool of individuals seeking to exchange Amazon gift card balances - which is done at a discount to face value - for Bitcoin. People end up with Amazon gift cards for many reasons other than as gifts, and for those folks who are 'unbanked' and living in a third-world country, exchanging a gift card balance for Bitcoin can make sense. Also, in an effort to improve the service, Purse.io has recently added ShapeShift to their platform, which means you can now use just about any of the major cryptos to make purchases.

Major Retailers Accepting Bitcoin (Just A Partial List Here)

Overstock.com
Expedia
eGift
New Egg
Dallas Mavericks
Shopify Stores
Dish
Roadway Moving
Intuit
Microsoft
Reeds Jewelers
Cheap Air
Subway (not all stores)
Gyft

SpendBitcoins.com provides a complete directory of retailers worldwide accepting Bitcoin. Another great resource to find local Bitcoin-friendly businesses is CoinMap.Org.

Unsurprisingly, you will find much wider Bitcoin acceptance in larger cities, as well as in areas that have an affinity for digital currency. IN NEW HAMPSHIRE, HOME TO THE LIBERTARIAN MOVEMENT, MANY BUSINESSES PREFER DIGITAL CURRENCY OVER THE DOLLAR. Major U.S. cities where you will find widespread acceptance of Bitcoin include Boston, Los Angeles, New York City, and San Francisco.

Overstock.com

Patrick Byrne, the CEO of Overstock.com, is a big supporter of the cryptocurrency movement. In 2014, he became the first major retailer to accept Bitcoin. In August 2017, it was reported that Overstock's board approved a plan to hold on to 50 percent of the Bitcoin payments it received. Most retailers that accept Bitcoin do so through a payment service that converts the payment to cash. In the case of Overstock, however, they have made the accumulation of Bitcoin part of their long-term business plan.

Byrne told Business Insider in February 2018 that his company has also invested millions of dollars in a new crypto venture called Ravencoin. I do not own any Ravencoin yet, but it is on my short list for consideration. For more information and to download the white paper, go to Ravencoin.org.

Bitcoin Debit Cards

Another way to deal with a Bitcoin 'denier' is to pull a Bitcoin-funded Visa or Mastercard from your wallet. If you happen to use Coinbase, there is a great Visa debit card option called the Shift

Card.

Other Crypto Debit Cards

Wirex (Wirexapp.com)

BitPay (Bitpay.com)

Cryptopay (Cryptopay.me)

HashCard (Hashcard.io)

Section Nine: Bitcoin Comes To Wall Street

How To Buy Bitcoin In A Brokerage Account (Including In An IRA)

One investment vehicle that has become very popular among Bitcoin enthusiasts is the Grayscale Bitcoin Investment Trust (symbol: GBTC). The trust, also popularly referred to as 'Bitcoin stock,' was initially formed as a private investment fund, available only to accredited investors. GBTC later gained approval to trade on the over-the-counter (OTC) market. Settling for a listing on the OTC is a way around the more arduous approval processes required by the major exchanges, such as the NYSE. Although the OTC market does not carry with it the credibility of a prominent exchange, anyone with a standard brokerage account can now buy shares of the trust, including inside of an IRA account.

While GBTC unquestionably provides a unique opportunity to investors, there's one wrinkle you should be aware of - the trust shares actually trade at a hefty premium to Bitcoin. What this means is that investors in the fund are paying considerably more for Bitcoin than its present value on the open market.

In 2017, the average premium of the fund was roughly 60 percent. This means that shareholders are paying an extra 60 cents for every dollar of Bitcoin they buy. Critics say that no one should be paying such an exorbitant premium, but many investors, recognizing the unique potential of a securitized Bitcoin opportunity, are fine with paying it. Still, while most analysts agree that a premium for a fund like this is not unusual, the 60-percent figure has understandably drawn widespread criticism.

Tracking The GBTC Premium

Investors in the trust must keep a close eye on the premium – yes, it fluctuates. I learned from experience that buying when the premium drops to 50 percent and selling when it reaches 60 percent works very well as a short-term trading strategy. A simple rule of thumb to keep in mind is that one share of GBTC equals approximately one-tenth of one percent of a Bitcoin.

As an example, a $10 share price for GBTC would represent an implied value of a single Bitcoin of $10,000 ($10,000 divided by 1,000). If the present market price of Bitcoin is only $6,500, the premium is $3,500 ($10,000 minus $6,500). As a percentage, THIS IS A 53-PERCENT PREMIUM OVER THE ACTUAL VALUE OF THE UNDERLYING ASSETS. Without having to do the math yourself, you can get the premium from the prior day's closing price from Bloomberg by doing a Google search for 'Bitcoin Trust Bloomberg.' The screenshot below shows a 65-percent premium for GBTC on May 11, 2018.

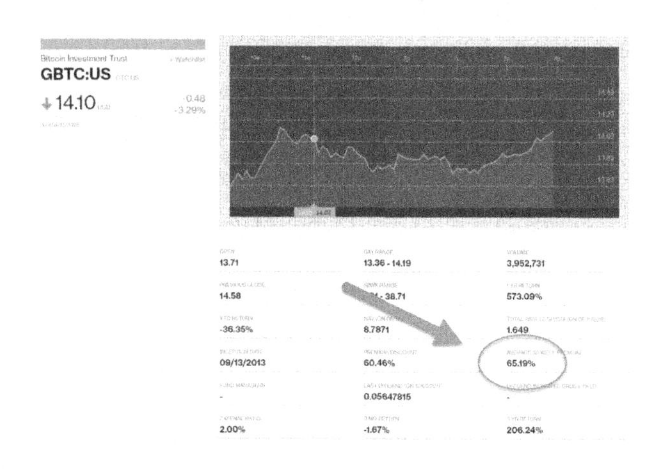

Who Is Right About The Premium?

Although many investors, including myself, are paying it, it's not likely that a 50- to 60-percent premium for GBTC is sustainable. The major sea change will undoubtedly occur when more Bitcoin investment funds enter the market. As additional options become available, the GBTC premium will inevitably be reduced. THIS COULD CREATE THE VERY UNUSUAL SCENARIO OF TRUST INVESTORS LOSING MONEY WHILE BITCOIN IS RISING IN PRICE.

One reason many investors are not concerned about the premium right now is that they are believers in a dramatically higher Bitcoin value. For example, if you are on the '$100,000 for Bitcoin' prediction bandwagon, you just don't care about paying an extra 60 cents on the dollar today. For many, it is no different from paying $1.60 for a one-dollar lottery ticket that offers the potential to win millions. The possibility of Bitcoin one day being worth six figures drives many investors to enthusiastically invest in GBTC despite the premium.

More Crypto Funds Coming From Grayscale

Grayscale recently announced the launch of four new funds: a Bitcoin Cash fund, a Litecoin fund, a Ripple fund, and an Ethereum fund. These will also start as private funds available only to accredited investors. Most likely, they will be listed on the OTC market within a year to 18 months after launch.

Other Than Buying The Grayscale Bitcoin Trust (GBTC), Are There Any Other Ways To Buy Cryptocurrency In An IRA?

THERE ARE SEVERAL SELF-DIRECTED CUSTODIANS NOW OFFERING THE OPTION OF OWNING BITCOIN DIRECTLY WITHIN AN IRA. Self-directed IRA custodians have been around for a long time.

These accounts allow individuals to buy more exotic investments than what is typically permitted in a traditional bank or brokerage IRA. Owning real estate, tax liens, and even physical gold coins within a self-directed IRA is possible.

In 2014, the IRS ruled that Bitcoin is to be considered property for tax purposes. Self-directed IRA custodians are relying on that ruling as the basis for embracing Bitcoin as an IRA-eligible asset. While I'm in no position to dispute their interpretations of the decision, it's likely we've not heard the last from the IRS about Bitcoin and IRA eligibility.

The IRS many times gives guidance on what assets are permitted in an IRA. In this case, however, I cannot find any solid evidence that the IRS has specifically approved cryptocurrency as an IRA asset. As a result, I am going to take a 'wait and see' approach with respect to crypto and IRA eligibility. THERE'S NO DENYING, HOWEVER, THAT IT WOULD MAKE MORE FINANCIAL SENSE TO BUY BITCOIN DIRECTLY WITHIN AN IRA, RATHER THAN PAYING A 60-PERCENT PREMIUM ON THE PURCHASE OF GRAYSCALE BITCOIN TRUST SHARES.

Section Ten: How To Get Bitcoin And Crypto Without Paying For It

There are a variety of ways to add to your crypto portfolio without parting with cold hard cash. In this chapter, I will share with you some of my favorite methods of accumulating crypto without spending a dime.

After reading this book, you may decide to start your *own* blog or website on the topic of cryptocurrency (just like I have done with BitcoinBloodhound.com). Listed below are a number of great options you can use to monetize your online presence. AFFILIATE COMPENSATION ARRANGEMENTS CHANGE FREQUENTLY. THE REFERRAL COMPENSATION DETAILS THAT FOLLOW ARE BELIEVED TO BE ACCURATE AT THE TIME OF PUBLICATION. THE READER SHOULD REVIEW THE MOST UP-TO-DATE AFFILIATE COMPENSATION DETAILS FOR EACH SITE PRIOR TO DECIDING TO PROMOTE ANY PRODUCT OR SERVICE.

Referral Programs

Affiliate arrangements offer a financial incentive to Internet marketers for promoting third-party products and services through referral links. The idea itself is not new, but being paid in cryptocurrency *is* a recent innovation. While some of the most popular crypto referral programs are listed below, you can find hundreds more by simply doing a Google search for 'Bitcoin referral program.'

Beware: As great as the potential is with crypto referral programs, this realm is swarming with scams. If you get involved with a fraudulent offer, you might unwittingly end up promoting an illegal operation. For example, I was recently approached about a Bitcoin multi-level marketing scheme. While I don't know for sure that it was actually a scam, several red flags came up when I started researching the company.

There are a lot of marketers trying to use Bitcoin to leverage weak business opportunities or even hatch outright scams. Even though, as an affiliate, you are not promoting your own product or service when you provide a referral, you may still have liability if it turns out the company is doing something illegal. This is why you should *always* perform excellent due diligence on every referral opportunity you consider. Additionally, besides doing research on a company, I make it a habit to use the product or service myself before promoting it on my website.

Federal Trade Commission Disclosure Requirements

To avoid legal problems when promoting referral links, you should also familiarize yourself with the FTC disclosure requirements for affiliate marketers. In a nutshell, you must fully disclose that you will receive compensation for your recommendations and endorsements. I recommend that you visit the FTC website (FTC.Gov) and do a search for 'FTC Endorsement Guides' for a complete overview of your legal responsibilities.

Coinbase

Coinbase has a program that pays $10 in Bitcoin for every new account you refer, once your referral makes a purchase of at least $100. Your referral *also* receives $10 in bonus Bitcoin. To make it easy to share this offer, I purchased the domain BitcoinBonus.US and forwarded it to my lengthier Coinbase referral link. Forwarding a domain is very simple to do inside the dashboard of your domain provider.

You can pick up a cheap domain from GoDaddy for less than $10. There are, of course, countless ways to promote your site. Promoting it through social media outlets, like Facebook and Twitter, remains among the best options, but you can also just mention your website in everyday conversations about Bitcoin, as well.

Purse.IO

I mentioned Purse.IO earlier – this is the website that provides discounts of up to 33 percent at Amazon when you pay with Bitcoin. With their affiliate arrangement, you can earn a varied referral fee for each new customer that uses the service. Just as I do with Coinbase, I have my own forwarding domain for Purse - SaveWithPurse.US

Another way to earn money from Purse.IO is by exchanging your own Amazon gift card balance for Bitcoin. To do this, click on the 'earn' button at the top of the Purse.IO home page. A great way to accumulate Amazon gift cards for this purpose is to join the Amazon Associates affiliate program. The program offers free enrollment and the opportunity to promote Amazon products on your own blog, website, or social media accounts. I have been an Amazon affiliate for more than a decade. Providing links to recommended books and other products has proved to be both a great income opportunity for me *and* a useful service to my readers.

Robinhood

The Robinhood app is a favorite among millennials. Users can invest small sums of money in the stock market *commission-free*, with no minimum deposit requirement. While the app is best known for stocks, no-fee Bitcoin and Ethereum trading is now available. The referral program pays one share of stock for each new account referred. I recently joined the program, and have already received several free shares of stock. Those I refer *also* receive a free share of stock. You might be given a share worth just a few dollars, or much more (the share you receive is selected at random). Presently there is a 1 in 200 chance of receiving a share of Berkshire Hathaway, Apple, or Facebook. So far I have received shares valued from $3 to $5 each. Up to this point, I have been cashing in all of my free stocks and using the proceeds to buy Bitcoin through the app. Feel free to use my affiliate link to qualify for your own free share of stock (FreeStocks.US).

CoinMama

CoinMama is a simple Bitcoin-buying platform that pays a 15-percent commission (ongoing) to customers you refer.

Trezor

Trezor is a hardware wallet manufacturer that pays up to 10 percent for referrals.

Ledger Wallet

Another hardware wallet manufacturer, Ledger Wallet pays 15 percent of the net sale amount on referrals (minus VAT and shipping charges).

KeepKey Wallet

This hardware wallet manufacturer offers a two-tier affiliate arrangement. Affiliates are paid $10 when they refer a sale, and a 10-percent override on affiliates they refer.

Accepting Crypto As Payment Yourself

If you are a business owner, you might want to consider accepting Bitcoin as a form of payment. You might even consider earmarking payments made in Bitcoin as savings, and hold on to it. As mentioned previously, Overstock.com retains fifty percent of Bitcoin payments as a long-term investment.

To begin accepting Bitcoin payments, simply provide your customers with your wallet receive address. Alternatively, many businesses will display their QR code at the cash register (or on their website). As discussed earlier, a QR code is simply a visual representation of your alphanumeric wallet address. To pay you, your customer would simply point their smart phone at your QR code and select the amount of Bitcoin to send.

You might also choose to work with a Bitcoin payment processor. A processor provides the same sort of service as credit card merchant accounts. The largest processing service is Bitpay. These services are designed to serve the business owner who wants to accept Bitcoin and have it immediately converted to cash.

Taking Crypto As A Donation Or Tip

Accepting Bitcoin as a tip or donation has become very popular for online content creators. If you have a following comprised largely of cryptocurrency users, you might want to consider posting your QR code with a call to action for crypto donations.

Love this site? Tip The Bloodhound!

Freelance Sites That Pay You In Bitcoin

If you're a freelancer and want to get paid in

Bitcoin, there are several platforms available that can assist you.

Cryptogrind (Cryptogrind.com)

XBT Freelancer (XBT Freelancer.com)
/r/Jobs4Bitcoins (Reddit group https://www.reddit.com/r/Jobs4Bitcoins/)
Changelly (Changelly.com)

A competitor to ShapeShift, Changelly is a coin-exchanging service. A coin-exchanging service provides the means to quickly convert a coin you own to another cryptocurrency. Changelly offers a 50-percent revenue share for life on customers you refer to their site.

Exchanges

Binance (Binance.com) - 20% of fees ongoing.
CEX (Cex.io) - 30% of fees ongoing.
Cryptopia (Cryptopia.com)
Local Bitcoins (LocalBitcoins.com) - A peer-to-peer exchange offering a 40% commission for three months.

Portfolio Management Tools

Coin Tracking (CoinTracking.info) 20 percent referral rate.
Coinigy (Coinigy.com) $15 for each paid

subscription.

What Is Mining, and Is It Profitable?

You won't need a pick, an ax, or a shovel to mine cryptocurrency. Mining provides a financial incentive for individuals to contribute computing power to a cryptocurrency network. Decentralized crypto networks like Bitcoin add transactions to the public ledger through the shared computing power of hundreds of thousands of CPUs worldwide (miners).

When I first learned about mining, I was thinking in terms of utilizing a single desktop computer. That may have been possible in the earliest stages of the Bitcoin evolution, but no more. THE LEVEL OF MINING DIFFICULTY HAS BECOME SIGNIFICANT, WITH THE EQUIPMENT REQUIREMENTS TO LAUNCH EVEN A MODEST BITCOIN MINING OPERATION RUNNING $10,000 AND HIGHER. Mining will continue to become increasingly competitive (and costly) as the remaining pool of available coins continues to diminish. It is unknown when the last Bitcoin will be mined, but most experts believe it could happen within just ten years.

Another challenge to mining has to do with the cost of electricity. The amount of power required to mine today is staggering. Most mining rigs are up and running 24/7 and consume significant electricity. As a result, mining is popular in areas with low electric rates. A recent article predicted that by the end of 2018, Bitcoin mining will consume as much electricity as the country of Austria! Since mining equipment produces a significant amount of heat, there is also more mining in colder climates. The idea of a computer generating free Bitcoin 24/7 sounds incredible, but today's world of crypto mining is now at an Olympic level.

A Modestly-Sized Mining Rig

Even if you live in a cool climate and have access to low-cost electricity, the profit margin in mining is still thin. WhatToMine.com is a site that provides tools to calculate mining profitability. I HAVE REPEATEDLY RUN THE NUMBERS, AND REMAIN CONVINCED THAT MINING IS AN IMPRACTICAL WAY TO ACCUMULATE BITCOIN. I

HATE TO BE THE SPOILER HERE, AND OPINIONS CERTAINLY VARY, BUT I JUST DON'T THINK MINING MAKES FINANCIAL SENSE TODAY. RATHER THAN SPENDING THOUSANDS OF DOLLARS ON MINING EQUIPMENT, USE THAT MONEY TO BUY MORE CRYPTO.

If you *do* decide to get into mining, note that most people enjoy greater success by joining a 'mining pool.' By combining your mining power with a 'pool' of other miners, your chances of earning more crypto will exponentially increase.

What Is Cloud Mining?

Rather than spending a small (or *not*-so-small) fortune on your own mining equipment, you can rent 'hashing power' on a large computer network. MANY CRITICS CONSIDER CLOUD MINING ARRANGEMENTS NOTHING MORE THAN PONZI SCHEMES - a way to collect large sums from investors and pay the money back in drips. If you want to try cloud mining yourself, the most popular service is Pool.Bitcoin.com.

News coverage on crypto mining is many times very negative, including reports of electricity theft and unauthorized use of computer networks. There are countless stories of people surreptitiously accessing electricity at their place of employment or college dorm, or clandestinely installing mining software on large computer networks. Consider this the new high-tech way to steal from your employer. One noteworthy example of this kind of power theft involved a government employee who used the computers of the Federal Reserve Bank to mine Bitcoin for two years before he was caught.

Cloud Mining Affiliate Programs

As mentioned previously, I am not really a fan of cloud mining, but if you feel differently, here is a list of cloud miners that you can promote and will pay you crypto.

Hashflare (Hasflare.io) - 10 percent referral commissions.
CCG Mining (CCG Mining.com) - 6 percent referral commissions.
Genesis Mining (Genesis-mining.com) - Sliding referral commission rate of 2.5 to 6 percent.

Earn Crypto By Blogging And Vlogging

I recently started a blog at Steemit.com (steemit.com/@jameslparis) and couldn't be happier. Steemit is a leader in the burgeoning decentralized social media movement. Decentralization is a growing trend; not just in the realm of cryptocurrency, but in the social media space, as well.

The site, and associated video platform, DTube, combine the concepts of social media and crypto. The company's founder, Dan Larimer, is also the creator of Bitshares, Steem, Steem Dollar and EOS. Steemit users earn cryptocurrency on the platform for both content creation and content curation. Earnings are based on the number of 'upvotes' received on blog and video posts (similar to Facebook likes). Users can earn even more by using their votes to help select the best content.

By now, you're probably aware of all the stories of people being censored on Facebook and YouTube. My YouTube account was demonetized several years ago, and I was given a well-publicized one-week suspension from Twitter in 2009. Facebook co-founder Mark Zuckerberg was recently called to testify before Congress about a wide host of issues, among them the censorship of conservative viewpoints. Talk show host Dennis Prager is presently suing YouTube for restricting his conservative content. Radio talk show host Alex Jones is in a constant battle with Facebook and YouTube over his content.

If you have strong opinions on politics, health issues, firearms, or religion, you may already be under siege from the small handful of social media platforms that control the Internet.

Decentralized social media eliminates the censors and middlemen in the way decentralized cryptocurrency eliminates the need for banks. Of course, decentralized sites have limits. Truly egregious and harmful content can be flagged and removed by the community of other users. While this is not a perfect way to moderate content, it's a much more libertarian approach than using jack-booted moderators. Steemit is a great alternative to Facebook and another way to generate free cryptocurrency.

Conclusion

I sincerely wish you the greatest of success on your cryptocurrency journey. In closing, I want to again encourage you to start small. As mentioned repeatedly in this book, you can make your first purchase with less than $100. When moving in this new direction, take baby steps. Even to this day, when I transfer a large amount of crypto, I do so piecemeal. Also, when in doubt, reach out for help. There are so many great resources and forums online, and there is no shortage of fellow travelers in the crypto community who are happy to help you. As an early adopter, be prepared to be the butt of a few jokes among your circle, but never forget that 'he who laughs last, laughs best'! Lastly, don't hold grudges against Bitcoin-deniers. Down the road, you should forgive your ignorant friends and family and allow them to visit you on your private island, because it's the right thing to do.

To your success!

Made in the USA
Monee, IL
11 July 2020

36393297R00090